REDEFINING FAMILY

A BIRTHMOTHER'S PATH TO WHOLENESS

A. K. SNYDER

First paperback edition January 2020

Cover design by Danna Mathias
"Love of Letting Go" music lyrics by Patty Kakac
"On Children" poem by Khalil Gibran

ISBN 978-0-578-61285-0 (paperback)
ISBN 978-0-578-61466-3 (ebook)

aksnyderbooks.com

Published by Wandering River Press
Tampa, Florida
wanderingriverpress.com

To Katarina,

May you know the whole story. May you feel, in your bones, that you are wanted and loved.

REGRET

"You'll regret it."

I heard it again and again.

I am not one to cling to regrets or to even allow myself to wonder "what if."

But now, eighteen years later, I will answer the question.

Do I regret it?

Do I regret getting pregnant at seventeen?

Do I regret carrying you through to delivery?

Do I regret placing you for adoption?

The answers do not come easily and cannot be given out of context.

You need the whole story.

PART I

BEFORE

1

DEREK

I am seventeen and I have met the love of my life.

He writes me poetry.

"Want to go to the library?" I ask my two-year-old niece.

She grins and pulls the stroller out of the closet. We have made this walk many times in the six months that I have lived with my sister, Joyce. I have not settled into this sprawling suburban high school, with more students than my home-town's population. The library offers a dose of the familiar. And internet.

Desiree flips through picture books while I get online and check my email.

New poems from Derek.

. . .

He doesn't write me love poems. Nothing so cliché.

No, his work is broody. Full of hurt and despair.

Like me.

His work examines the world, our society. Peels back layers and diagnoses the dark side of our being. I am fascinated with his perspective.

I have told no one my secrets.

Why I live with my sister now.

Why I won't see my father.

Why I feel alienated and alone.

These things are all too big, too hard to look at, too much for me right now.

I focus on getting by. Head down, do the work, put in the effort, and keep moving forward. I can't stop now or I fear I'll never move forward again.

But Derek. Derek makes me think maybe I can do both.

Maybe I can start to look at these experiences through a poet's lens and unravel them in slices. Maybe they won't destroy me. Maybe I can find happiness this way.

Derek makes me feel like I will be okay someday.

I am in love.

Desiree tires of her books. She climbs back into her stroller.

We stop at the grocery store on the way home. Dried papaya for her. Sugary iced tea for me. And milk. I was supposed to get milk. I hang the plastic bag with a gallon of milk from the handle of the stroller and walk home.

2

MOVING OUT

For the last six months, I've shared a room with my niece, while my sister and her husband, Matt, worked mad hours trying to make a home for their kid plus me, an unexpected tenant who doesn't pay rent.

I like living with Joyce and Matt, but I am missing out.

I tried to fit into this overwhelming school of thousands.

I never found my footing.

And now it is summer and I am alone.

I picture my old friends hanging out at the dock, around bonfires, in basement family rooms watching movies and making inside jokes.

Without me.

Plus, Derek lives in my hometown now, and he's friends with my old friends, my group before I moved out, before my life changed.

I tell Joyce I'm going back.

Mom says I can live with her.

But she and my little brother, Mark, are just starting to make it. They are staying in my uncle's house, across the driveway from Grandma, on the farm where Mom grew up.

Grandma helps as much as she can. A cousin down the road takes Mark sometimes. She has a son who is also around ten years old and they play well together.

If I move back in with them, I'll disrupt their tenuous stability.

I used to be responsible for Mark. Take him with me when I worked at the grocery store. He would shoot hoops at the community center until I bought us lunch. Ritz crackers and a jar of peanut butter. Then I would go back to work and he would hang out until my shift ended. I brought him everywhere with me. Bought our food, made our plans.

But now, he has adults caring for him again. I don't want to mess with that.

Plus, I want to be a little irresponsible.

I want to run off with Derek.

See the graffiti gardens he talks about.

Read poetry and listen to music.

Lie in the grass and talk about possibilities, endless possibilities.

I tell Mom I'm staying at my friend, Julia's, but Julia's parents would never go for this.

I'll figure something out.

3

CRASHING

Derek knows a place.

He and his buddy have been crashing here for the last few months. He says I can stay.

I tell him I need a job first, so I can pay rent.

"No rent," he says. He has beautiful thick eyelashes and a mischievous grin. He shows me the place.

A two-story building on Main Street, a bar on the main level. The second story is empty. I think there was once a fire here.

We climb up the back fire escape and crawl through a broken window. There are no walls, only studs. The sunlight casts a yellow tinge, dust particles caught in the air. It smells of old wood and young men.

A raggedy couch.

A futon.

A gallon jug of water next to a cooler.

"You live here?" I ask.

"For now."

Life is not about the endless accumulation of wealth and stuff. It's about art and thought and poetry and music and love. Derek and I have spent hours discussing these things. And here, I would have freedom. And I would have Derek.

"Where do you go to the bathroom?"

"Gas station." He points out the window to the station across the street. "They're open until ten. The laundry mat," he moves to another window, "is open all night, and you can wash up in the bathroom there and no one cares. Huge bathrooms."

There's no electricity, but who needs it? The sky should be dark at night, so we can see the stars and recognize how small we are, how small our troubles are, how infinite everything else is.

"Can I see the roof?"

"That's my favorite place." He takes my hand. We crawl out a different window and scramble to the roof.

Yes, I could live here.

He pulls me into his arms and I am happy.

4

TWENTY-FOUR

Derek is twenty-four.

I am seventeen.

"Don't you see," Mom says, "there's something wrong with that? Why does he want to date a girl so young?"

"I'm not a child!" I say. "I'm very mature! And what's so wrong with me? Why shouldn't he love me? He loves me!"

He is twenty-four.

I am seventeen.

And I see nothing wrong with that.

5

SHRUG

Six months later, we sit on the hood of the car, Derek and I, waiting for our friend to emerge from the store.

"What if we got pregnant?" I ask him.

He shrugs.

"I'd probably give it to my sister, Joyce," I say.

"Why not get an abortion?" he asks.

I shrug.

I don't think that's right for me, but I can't explain why. My feminist side won't regurgitate pro-life arguments, but I also know that's not the right path for me.

Our friend returns. "Ready?"

We shrug. "Let's go."

6

FIGHT

Derek and I fight a lot.

Alone, we have fun. He is sweet and compassionate, and I adore him.

But with others, he is distant and dark. He pulls me away, back into our own circle of two.

If I have fun without him, if I make him feel left out, I have to spend the next couple of days reassuring him that things are okay. I try to include him, but he doesn't join. Doesn't want to be included.

He says I am different around my friends.

And I know he's right.

I go back to an old version of myself. A happier version.

A shallower, younger version.

A version of me he doesn't like.

We fight and make up.

We break up and make up.

And eventually, I decide this isn't going to work for me.

7

NEWS

"I think I know why you've been feeling so lousy," the doctor says. "You're pregnant."

I say nothing.

"Do you know who the father is?" she asks.

"Yes. My boyfriend. Well, my ex-boyfriend now. But we're still friends." As though that matters to her.

"I can't be pregnant," I say. "I'm going to college next week. Doing my senior year at St. Cloud State."

The doctor nods. "What do you want to do?"

"I want to take another test," I say. "I want a different result."

"There is a blood test we could do, but the one you took is

98% accurate. And it fits with you feeling tired all the time, and nauseous, and sensitive to smells."

I can't swallow.

"Can I get you something?" she asks. "Water maybe?"

Mom drove me here. She is out in the lobby waiting for me. I cannot go out there and tell her this news.

"Yeah, water please," I say. "And maybe a minute alone? Do you have a pen and paper?"

She fetches a paper cup of ice-cold water and a branded pharmaceutical pad of paper. "I'll be back in a few minutes."

I scrawl my panic onto the paper. My letters grow large and loopy. I write out my plan. Or as much of a plan as I can think through at this moment.

The words are a mess, but my head stops swimming.

Today, I need to pull myself together. Just keep it together. I need to tell Derek before I tell anyone else.

When the doctor comes back, I tear off the sheets and shove them in my back pocket.

"Do you know what you're going to do?"

"I'm going to give her up for adoption," I say.

Her face is soft and sad. "I'd like to see you back again in the next couple weeks, then. Talk about prenatal vitamins and make a plan together."

"I can't. I'm going to college next week. Moving to St. Cloud."

"They have medical staff on site at the college. It's important to start seeing a doctor regularly, especially early in the pregnancy."

I nod, take a deep breath, and try to cover my face in calm.

Mom puts down the waiting room magazine. "What did she say?"

"Just nerves," I say.

8

GRANDMA

I am pregnant.

I am seventeen, a senior in high school, on my own, and headed to early college in a week.

And I am pregnant.

I refuse to be a statistic.

I will not drop out of school.

I will not end up a distracted mom of four kids from four dads, all of us living on welfare, going nowhere.

I will not fail.

I am going to tell Derek today.

He doesn't have a job, so no problem getting him to connect

with me on a random weekday afternoon. But he also doesn't have a car, so we invite our friend Shelly.

"Want to go to those beautiful gardens in St. Cloud? The ones we drive by and never visit?"

She's game and happy to drive.

While I'm waiting for them to show up, I remember I was supposed to get Grandma's mail. I run to the mailbox, then take her letters across the driveway to her house and let myself in.

"Hi Grandma. I have your mail."

Grandma comes out from the bedroom smelling of Icy Hot. "Oh, thank you."

She stops and looks at me.

I must be wearing my anxiety on my face again.

"Are you okay?" she asks.

I nod, but suddenly tears and panic and fear clog my throat. Damn it. I need to get through today.

"When do you leave for school?"

"Next week."

"I have a little something for you," she says. "Hold on." She shuffles into her bedroom and returns with an envelope. I know she hasn't a dime to spare, but I cannot reject the offer.

"This isn't necessary," I say. "The high school pays for my college this year."

She just pats my hand. "It's necessary," she says.

I thank her and hug her and tuck it away unopened.

A few minutes later, standing in the driveway waiting for Derek and Shelly, I open the envelope.

A hundred-dollar bill and a sticky note. "For the little one. :)"

I have no idea how she knows.

9

DEREK

Shelly pumps gas. Derek and I are alone in the car.

"I went to the doctor yesterday," I say.

He looks at me, ice blue eyes. "And?"

I can't choke out the word.

I don't have to.

He looks at my stomach, then back at my eyes.

I nod.

Before he says anything, Shelly is back in the car and we are off to the well-tended gardens in full bloom.

10

BLOOM

Derek and Shelly and I walk through gilded trails, purples and reds and oranges in full August splendor. It is the end of the season's flowers and the air is thick with their scent.

We don't tell Shelly, but she senses something is up. She takes her camera and heads off on her own for a while, then returns. Then off again and back again.

Derek and I talk in the gaps.

"What do you want to do?" he asks.

"Give it up," I say.

"That's a relief," he says. "If you want to get married, I mean, when you turn eighteen, I would do that. I don't mind helping you raise it. Or I could help you pay for an abortion. Just don't expect me to pay child support. I won't do that."

What a charming offer.

. . .

"Thanks," I say.

"Are you still moving to St. Cloud?" he asks.

"Yeah."

"I got a job there," he says. "I start next week, at a restaurant. I could probably get you a job, too."

"That would be great. I haven't found anything yet."

"I'm a supervisor. I hope you don't mind if I'm your boss. But I could help take care of you. If you're sick or something, or have a doctor appointment, I could cover for you."

"Yeah, good. That would be good."

Shelly takes photos of Derek and me in cheesy poses, holding hands on a park bench, poking our heads through a vine-covered arbor.

He knows now.

And he's not going to fight me on the adoption or try to keep it himself.

And he's offered to help me using the small amount he has to offer.

It's as good as I could hope for today.

11

LOST

I am pregnant.

Joyce is also pregnant.

That day in the parking lot, when we talked about what I would do if I got knocked up, and I said I would give it to Joyce, it never occurred to me that she could be pregnant at the same time.

What if she decides she can't handle two babies?

What if she won't take mine?

I have no back-up plan.

I have no idea what I would do.

She has to take this baby. She has to. There has to be a way.

I call to tell her I am pregnant.

But her voice is wrong. Something is wrong.

"Are you okay?" I ask.

No, she is not okay.

She went to the doctor today. Her baby has no heartbeat.

At fifteen weeks, she's not sure if it was a boy or a girl. She named the baby Casey, her lost little one.

She is heartbroken.

I do not tell her. Not right now.

"I'm so sorry," I say.

I am certain I killed her baby.

My longing. My desperation. My determined focused desire to clear a space in this world for my baby destroyed Joyce's child, cleared her womb and her heart, and it is all my fault.

"I am so sorry," I repeat.

12

SICK

I cannot live in the dorms at the college because I'm too young. I thought I would be able to find a cheap apartment off-campus, but no one will rent to a seventeen-year-old, and the apartments are way more expensive than I expected. I find a cheap horrible efficiency, the kind willing to illegally rent an apartment to an underage kid.

It's an upgrade for me. It has plumbing and electricity.

The landlord is a decent guy. He walks me through the building and tells me which units house guys I need to avoid. I don't ask why I need to avoid them. I just thank him for the information.

I use my entire restaurant paycheck to cover the rent.

I throw up.

Every day. Many times a day. For months.

I drop from 135 pounds to 102. The doctor says she'll admit me if I can't keep myself hydrated.

I live on free meals from the restaurant and Slimfast shakes. The shakes my doctor recommended, a cheap and easy way to get some vitamins in me, and I can usually keep them down.

I do well in my classes, when I make it in, but I am so sick I miss about half. I keep up on the readings, and I learn things easily. I show up for tests, even if I throw up before, during, and after them.

When the state finally approves some food money through WIC, I can buy peanut butter and cheese and milk and cereal. I can't keep most of these things down, but the cereal helps a little.

13

ABORTION

Derek's buddy, the one who lived with us above the bar, walks me home from my shift at the restaurant.

"You don't have to do this, you know," his buddy says. "You don't have to be pregnant."

"I already told you, I don't want an abortion."

"Maybe think of it more like an intentional miscarriage. You just aren't ready for a baby. So tell your body you aren't ready for a baby, and if you want, I can get you some herbs to help. Or a doctor. There are things you can do."

I don't say anything.

"You're never going to make it, Alycea. At least not much above where you're at now. This is going to break you. Your emotional level, your psychological level will always be piss poor. You will never recover from this."

This friend of ours, he offered to help me get an abortion before. Many times before.

And not just him.

My friends.

My friends' parents.

They've all offered.

If I need a ride.

If I need the money.

There's no reason to walk this terribly difficult path, they tell me. You don't know what you're in for, they tell me. It will be harder than you think, they say.

Every week for the first few months, someone tries to convince me I am making the wrong decision.

It is always out of love. Out of compassion.

They are so certain that they could make my life easier, if I would only listen to them.

But I don't feel loved.

. . .

I feel so very alone.

I can't listen to them. Because I listen to you.

I feel you.

You are me and I am you.

You are not a decision I get to make.

You are something else. You belong here. You belong in this world.

I can't explain it.

I don't fight them on politics. I'm not an advocate for any side.

I am only an advocate for you.

It takes me three months to tell my Mom and siblings about you. Three months to find the words. And then I learn to lean toward family.

My sisters, my mom, they help me navigate.

No trying to convince me to do something else. No challenging my path. Just support.

My older brother, disappointed in my news, wraps me in acceptance and caring and "let me know how I can help" and "if there's anything at all I can do."

My little brother, eager to help, eager to show me love and make me laugh.

Family.

I wish one of them lived here, in this city with me.

I wish I could afford the long-distance bill so I could talk to them, get a shot of support from them every day.

But it is just me here.

And I am so very alone.

But for you.

14

COLLAPSE

I have a message from Joyce. "Call me when you get a chance."

My hand shakes as I call. I'm going to throw up again. She's had a week to think about it. Will she and Matt adopt this baby?

"No," she says.

I'm sure her words are kind, but I do not hear them.

I'm sure she gives me reasons, but her voice is swallowed by the sound of everything collapsing around me, the dreams I've built, the visions I've conjured.

. . .

The images of holidays where my child, happy and healthy and part of the family, runs into my arms and yells "Aunt 'Lycea" and it feels like home and safety and love.

The dust of the collapse burns my eyes. Tears stream.

"I gotta go," I say.

I hang up the phone, slide down the wall, and sob.

From a depth I didn't know I had. From the weakest, most terrified vulnerable parts of me, I sob.

And I do not stop.

15

ETIQUETTE I

There is no book of etiquette around adoption, but there should be.

"Do you know who the father is?"

Doctors ask, which seems fair.

But so does everyone else. Unconnected coworkers. Professors. Classmates who I've barely interacted with and with whom I have no friendly relationship.

Yes, I know who he is.

I didn't have to sleep with every guy in town to get knocked up.

One. Just one.

And yes, I know who he is. My boyfriend.

Was my boyfriend. Before we broke up.

But fuck you!

He's the only man I've ever been with and I loved him and he loved me and now I'm pregnant and you're a judgmental prick who can go to hell.

"There were just so many," I say, shaking my head.

16

DEREK'S PLACE

Derek looks out for me at work. He covers for me when I leave the floor mid-shift and bolt for the bathroom. He covers my shifts when I can't get up, can't get out of bed, can't walk the six blocks through the snow and cold to make six dollars an hour as a hostess at a cheap restaurant.

He doesn't like when I walk home from the restaurant after midnight, and I don't really like it either. Most nights, I wait for his shift to end and we walk to his place together. He lives in a slightly-less-sketchy efficiency. He has a futon that sleeps two. And he has a computer with internet access. I spend most of my time there.

We are not together anymore. There is no future for us and neither of us pretend there is.

. . .

But I need him.

Or, I need someone.

And he is willing to be that someone. For now.

When I get a craving and think I may be able to keep some-thing down, he walks to the grocery store. Oranges. Mint ice cream. Anything to stop me from throwing up all the time.

I know this isn't working. I am failing, not at school, but at life. I don't know what else to do.

I can't work more hours and keep up with classes.

I don't want to be a high school drop-out.

I have to pay rent.

I am failing.

And I don't know what else to do.

FORUMS I

I look for help online.

The internet forums around adoption are stuffed with trauma, tragedy, heart-wrenching stories.

Wounds that never heal, scabs that are picked at until they re-open, a daily reminder of the connections, severed bloodlines, bleeding for lifetimes.

The happy adoptees are not here. They are off living happy lives.

The birthparents at peace are not here. They are off living peaceful lives.

The settled adopted parents are not here. They have busy households and soccer practice and dinner to cook.

They may all pop in from time to time, but none linger.

. . .

The internet forums are for the rest of us, the frightened pregnant girls trying to make a plan, the open adoptions suddenly slammed closed, without warning, without explanation, the babies snatched away from loving adoptive parents after weeks, months, years of dedicated parenting.

The forums are a place of heartbreak.

But there is nowhere else to go, no one else to learn from.

Night after night, I sift through the posts and try to tell myself this is only part of the story.

Happy adoptions exist.

They must.

I go to the forums to find the mistakes to avoid so that, someday, I am not someone who lingers around these internet forums.

18

JUMPER

At a thrift store, I find a tiny baby girl outfit. A sea-foam green jumper with a pink flower on the belly, a summer outfit, perfect for a baby who will be born in April.

It is a dime. I buy it.

Somehow, this little outfit makes you feel more real. The fetus pictures I look at online, the Lennart Nilsson photographs that show me an alien now the size of a bean, now a walnut, now with ears. It is hard to connect those photographs with the spirit I feel inside me.

But this little green jumper with a flower on the tummy allows me to see you, a baby, as you will be in April or May.

I don't know what I'm going to do with it. Maybe send it with you, give it to the parents, whoever they will be. But for now, I tuck it away. I tell no one I bought this. They will think I plan to keep you, and I cannot explain otherwise.

19

OPEN

I want an open adoption. I want to see you.

I don't need to see you all the time. I don't want to disrupt your family life.

But the more I read about the negative effects of adoption, the abandonment and shame and disconnection that adoptees feel, the severed ties and the lingering sense of loss, the Primal Wound as the books refer to it, the more I feel this can be alleviated through just one open line of communication, one connection, one un-severed thread that binds the birthparent to the child, to anchor you, to root you, to help you know you were never forgotten or lost or unwanted.

You came before I was able to take good care of you.

That is all.

· · ·

I want that line, that tie, so I can send that message repeatedly through the years, through your ages, through your stages of development, as new questions appear and you wonder again if maybe I just didn't want you. I want that unbroken tie to sound out the message on repeat.

You are loved.

Wanted.

And cared for.

In the very best way I know how to do it.

And so I delve into open adoptions and try to learn how to set one up that provides enough security to your parents so they do not hold back, so they go all in with their love for you, but also enough connection to me so you don't feel lost in this world.

20

HEARTBEAT

Every check-up, I look forward to hearing that heartbeat.

Whoosh-whoosh-whoosh. Happy growing baby.

Today, there is no heartbeat.

The doctor adjusts the wand, adds more lube, tries another position.

No heartbeat.

I have an ultrasound scheduled for tomorrow.

21

ULTRASOUND

Whoosh-whoosh-whoosh.

All that throwing up, all that dehydration, and you are magically still okay.

I love the *whoosh-whoosh-whoosh* sound of your heart. On your first ultrasound, I can see it, your wild heartbeat, the source of that beautiful rhythm. Whoosh-whoosh-whoosh, in black and white, a tiny pulse, impossibly tiny.

I am so relieved I'm shaking. You are okay. You are still growing.

"Here's the brain," the technician says. "That's how you know it's a girl."

She laughs, then adds, "I never get to tell that joke!"

. . .

I realize that it's rare for a woman to have an ultrasound alone. I hadn't considered inviting anyone. Who would I bring with me?

No, I am in this alone. Check-ups, ultrasounds, and probably delivery, too. I just have to befriend some nurses when I go into labor and hope they will help me through it.

It's just you and me, kid.

FORUMS II

The forums are full of horror stories.

"They promised an open adoption. The day I signed the papers, they disappeared. I haven't heard from them in fourteen years. I don't know if he's dead or alive."

"They agreed to an open adoption, but my last letter was returned and their phone has been disconnected. The agency won't tell me anything. I have no idea what happened! Is she hurt? Is she dead? Why won't anyone respond to me?"

"They promised visits, but when I tried to schedule them, they were always too busy. I get one letter a year."

"They promised letters. They disappeared."

. . .

That's the thing about open adoptions. Only the "adoption" part is binding. The "openness" is merely a suggestion and all power goes to the new parents.

Birthparents, stand down.

You have given away your rights.

You have given up.

Now give up.

Sometimes, there is good reason.

Birthparents who add instability and confusion to the child's world. But most often, I suspect, the reasons are social pressure to normalize the family structure. Hurt, fear, jealousy closes the door more than anything else, I suspect.

I have little power to prevent these horror stories from happening to me, but I can do a something.

First, find a tough mom. Her strength will hold that door open.

Find a loving, committed dad. His support will keep this relationship okay.

And then, spend the rest of my life tip-toeing.

Don't make too much noise.

Don't offend.

Don't overstep.

Don't push.

Don't demand.

Always, always, they can close the door, change the rules.

They hold all the power.

Staying silent, polite, and in the background has never been my way. But maybe, if the stakes are high enough, I can learn.

I must learn.

The power is not mine. And the stakes are high enough.

23

FORUMS III

I add a new forum post to adoptees. "What mistakes did your birthparents make? I am five months pregnant and trying to figure out my adoption plan. I would like to know so I can try to structure this adoption as well as possible."

I am unprepared for the response.

I expected impassioned grievances and heartbreak, the kind of responses that would require me to sift through the pain to find the advice.

I received:

"This is such a thoughtful question. We would love to give a home to a child from a birthmother like you. We are a happily married couple from Boise…"

· · ·

"How would you like to structure your adoption? My husband and I are willing to work with any request, large or small, if you would consider us…"

"Are you still looking for adoptive parents? Joe and I have adopted three children, and all have very different relationships with their birthparents. If you would consider giving us your baby…"

"Please give us your baby."

"Give us a baby."

"Any baby."

I close the thread.

24

AGENCIES

I research adoption agencies. I hate them all.

Plastic white families, mothers in yellow cardigans with small cross necklaces, holding perfect white babies. The message throughout all the literature, buried in kind words, tells me "God doesn't want you to keep your baby."

But I need to find a family for this baby.

I don't trust this fourteen billion dollar industry.

Not one bit.

But I trust lawyers less.

On Derek's computer, I scroll through local agencies. I pretend

I want to adopt, want to set up an open adoption, and I look at the messaging they show to adoptive parents. I eliminate most agencies immediately based on their negative portrayals of birthparents and their image of adoptive parents shielding and saving these children from a tragic start in life. The parents who are drawn to that marketing are not the ones for my adoption plan.

Some agencies cost $50,000, some cost $10,000. I am looking for a stable family, not just a rich one, so I lean toward the lower-cost agencies.

I call a couple of agencies and ask about their birthparent services. Ask about their common arrangements.

"Do you do a lot of open adoptions?"

"Oh yes, open adoptions are standard now. We really think it's best for everyone involved."

"So you have birthmothers who visit the family?"

"Oh absolutely. We think everyone should have a chance to meet in person before the placement."

"I mean after the adoption. You have birthmothers who visit the families after the placement?"

"Oh goodness no. That would be very invasive. That's not what an open adoption is. With an open adoption, the parents will send letters and photos annually to the birthparents, but there's no in-person relationship after placement. That would be so confusing for the child."

I keep calling.

I find one agency that says they have some birthparents who visit the children, although they never recommend this arrangement. But if I can find parents who are open to it, they would be willing to work through the details with me.

I know how desperate these parents are. I am confident I can find a couple who will work with me.

I can't be the only person who thinks contact is a good idea. There has to be more open-minded parents out there. I just need to get past the gatekeepers.

25

PROFILES

The adoption agency lady pulls out a stack of files. She is going to help narrow them down for me.

Only households which already have children.

Local Minnesotan families.

Preferably with a mom who has a good career. I don't care about her salary, but I want a lifestyle where both parents are valued and share power in the home and this is the best way I know to screen for that.

I flip through the pages, scrapbooks designed to show the best versions of their lives.

I cringe at books that include only posed photographs, children in matching shirts and mom and dad in matching fake smiles.

I lean toward books stuffed with messy children, laughing candids, and oversized holiday banquets.

But always lingering in my mind is this couple I know.

They are trying to adopt. I would never give my child to them, would never add a baby to their dysfunction. And this couple would look ideal on paper. If their profile showed up in this stack, and I didn't know them, it is the one I would likely choose.

And that idea terrifies me.

26

FORUMS IV

To adoptees: "What mistakes did your birthparents make? I would like to know so I can structure my adoption plan as well as possible. If you are looking to adopt, please do not post here. I am only interested in responses from adoptees right now."

The most common response:

"She gave me away. She should have kept me."

Page after page, post after post.

"She should have kept me."

27

SNOWSTORM

A snowstorm shuts down Christmas Eve. Stores lock up at four in the afternoon. Buses stop running at four-thirty.

I trudge into my single-room efficiency, stomp snow off my boots, cold, with an aching belly.

Joyce calls. She can't make it tonight. The snow is too thick, the roads too slick.

Damn. I try more water, but it does not quiet the ache.

I haven't had a shift at the restaurant in four days, which means no free meals. Two days ago, I ran out of potato flakes, the kind you get in a box for eighty-eight cents and can turn into a full belly with nothing but hot water.

Yesterday, I drank my last Slimfast shake.

Today, I ate nothing.

I am more nauseous than hungry.

But the baby. The baby, grown five months in my belly, needs food.

I was to have a full meal tonight, a family meal, at Joyce's. Noodles and meat and tomatoes and cheese and maybe garlic bread.

But the snow has trapped her there and me here, and I'm going to be sick again. Stomach acid churning with nothing to digest.

I have a pound of ground deer meat in the freezer, the last of a gift from Mom's friend.

At the thought of it, I retch. I spit acid into the dirty toilet I share with my adjoining neighbor. I rinse my mouth and try more water.

Well, baby, here's your proof.

If it were up to me alone, we'd both starve.

I am not making it on my own.

I have no illusions that this would somehow get easier by adding an infant.

I have to put food in me or I'm going to starve this baby.

I pull the frost burnt venison from the freezer and swallow a mouthful of bile. Maybe if I could just turn it into a burger.

. . .

The guys across the hall are laughing. I've never said more than a passing hello to them, but I've also never wanted to call the cops on them, so that's a point in their favor.

Maybe they have bread, and ketchup.

Something to help me swallow this.

I knock.

A skinny guy, maybe twenty, opens the door. His buddy holds a video game remote. The smell of fried chicken smacks me.

"Sorry to interrupt on Christmas Eve." I am suddenly aware of my vomit breath and greasy hair. "I was wondering if you might have some bread and ketchup? The stores closed before I could get there. I can cook up a burger for you if you want. Maybe you'd be willing to trade me some bread for it."

I feel like a Dickens character. "Please sir, may I have some bread?"

Pathetic.

"Come in."

The buddy nods. "Hey."

"Hey." My movements, a nervous bird.

"You want chicken?" the guy asks. "I'll make you a plate."

"I don't want to take your dinner."

"We have more than enough." He does not wait for yes. He fills a paper plate with fried chicken, corn, potatoes, and cheese biscuits. More food than I've eaten all week. "Here."

"Thanks." My voice, a mouse squeak.

He gives me a sad smile.

"Merry Christmas."

28

CHANGE

Over Christmas, I talk to Mom. She wants me to live with her. Although I have not told my family exactly how bad things have gotten, I cannot lie to myself. I know that I am failing on my own. And I don't see how you and I are going to make it unless something big changes.

Mom and Mark have found a rhythm together now. Life is okay for them. Mom's divorce is finalized, and she has a little money. She wants to help.

Since I'm still a senior, my high school is paying for this year of college. I'm not sure what will happen if I move to a new school district. Maybe the tech school in Mom's town is an option.

It's my sister, Rachel, who convinces me. She thinks her boyfriend might be cheating on her. Which means that she knows but isn't ready to admit it yet until she's figured out her plan.

She thinks she might leave him, but then what? Where would she live? What would she do?

"What if we both move in with Mom for a while?" I ask her. "You could be my Lamaze person."

Her relationship with Mom is even more strained than mine, but Mom is different these days. Trying to change things with us. Trying to change things for herself.

And we would have each other.

I don't want to have this baby alone.

I don't want to grieve this baby alone.

Rachel by my side, this could make all the difference in the world.

She agrees. We'll both move in with Mom and Mark.

29

HOME

After Christmas, six months pregnant and a hundred pounds, broke and broken, I move in to Mom's house.

It is warm and feels like home.

Rachel moves in, too. She leaves the cheating boyfriend and we gather in this new place.

Everything about this arrangement shows our lives in limbo.

Mom, figuring out how to be single, exploring what life might be now that she's free from a twenty-year abuse sentence.

Rachel, twenty-three, newly single and working her way out of heartache.

And Mark. Eleven. Thrilled his sisters moved home. Happy to be living on the farm, Grandma across the way, siblings in the living room.

·   ·   ·

It's an odd arrangement and a good one. A few months to turn toward family.

We will help each other through the next few months.

It is good here.

Rachel and I sleep in the living room. There is not really space for us, but we create some anyway.

Since I am pregnant, I get the couch.

Rachel takes the loveseat, her feet hanging over the edge as she sleeps.

Every night, the four of us gather in the living room. I balance a bowl of ice cream on my belly and watch it jump as you wake up. Our routine. I stretch and you wake and tumble and twist inside me.

We watch reruns of Friends, Golden Girls, Frasier. Shows that had lost their humor when I watched them alone regain their punch lines when surrounded with family.

Every evening, we laugh. We take a few hours away from the trying and the striving, the worrying and the planning. Instead, we laugh. I fall asleep mid-episode, happy and fed, every night.

30

SISTERS

I have two sisters.

One who will walk with me through this.

Step by step. Through questions and worries, reruns and laughter, she will be my partner in the birthing classes and my support during delivery. She will stay by my side through every moment, hard or easy, laugh or cry.

The other preserves my sanctuary.

She will be my safe place to land. When my belly and heart are empty, I will go to her, find refuge in her home, and she will help me heal.

I shelter between them and thank the universe for giving me two sisters.

31

PRIEST

Mom wants me to talk to her priest.

He has helped her before, when she was stuck, when she was ashamed, when she needed to leave my father but feared she would be branded a bad Catholic and a bad wife and a bad mother, and he told her God never meant for her to be in an abusive relationship and that is not a marriage.

I know this is hard for her, watching me hurt.

I know this is embarrassing for her, to be the mom of the pregnant teenager.

She is stepping up anyway.

She will feel better if I talk to her priest.

We enter his cramped church office, stamping boots and removing mittens.

"Hello, Father."

Five greyhounds follow his every move. Old dogs. Race dogs who found sanctuary in his home, to live out their final days. He shoos them out and closes the door.

He skips the small talk. "How far along are you?"

"Six months."

"Do you have a plan?"

"I'm going to give her up for adoption."

"Have you selected a family?"

"No."

Then he asks Mom if he can speak to me alone.

The door lets in cold air from the hallway when she leaves.

He looks at me, blue eyes gentle and lined. "Is your plan adoption because that is what you want to do, or because you feel like you don't have any options?"

I am caught off-guard.

"If you want to keep your baby, Alycea, I will help you. We can get you on food stamps, find subsidized housing. You do not have to give your baby away just because you don't have money, or because someone else thinks you should."

I have no words.

He lets that silence open wide and encompass the space between us.

"That's not the only reason," I say. I do not share my reasons. At this moment, I have forgotten them.

"I am sure," I say.

He nods, but allows the silence enough time to invite contradictions.

I do not waver.

Comfortable in my response, he offers to invite Mom back in.

He knows a family, parishioners, who would very much like to adopt. He asks thoughtful questions.

"What kind of adoption are you arranging?"

"What level of contact do you want?"

I assume he did his research beforehand, as there is no book of etiquette, and he does not assume or ask anything offensive.

Perhaps if you spend a lifetime practicing love and kindness and acceptance, you don't need a rule book on how to treat people well. If I were to say this, I bet he would tap his Bible and assert that he already has a rule book, and a Santa Claus twinkle would appear in his eye. Maybe it's the heat in this tiny room, but the meeting takes on a surreal shimmer.

He says my answers are very similar to his parishioners' answers. "Think about it. Later, if you want, I can arrange a meeting, or perhaps provide you with their phone number and you can call when you're ready."

I've been to pro-life clinics, where I was shamed and guilted and smothered in agenda.

I've been to pro-choice clinics, where I was insulted and chastised and, again, smothered in agenda.

But this rural Catholic priest offered more authentic caring and support than any clinic which claimed to be there to support me.

32

FORUMS V

I read more horror stories.

Not on purpose. I am on the internet forums again, reading adoptees' stories.

The birthmother signed away her rights, but then, later, they learned the baby had a heart condition and all those warm welcoming adoptive homes locked their doors. Those doors only open for healthy babies.

The birthmother planned to give her up, but she was born with a previously undetected anomaly. Once again, the homes disappeared. Like Avalon, they only appear for the worthy infants, and any sub-par physical or mental condition makes kids unworthy.

. . .

I don't hate adoptive parents for this. Adoption is expensive and few can afford more than one. And not all parents are equipped to be special needs parents. I would also argue that most parents don't choose to be special needs parents; they grow into it through devotion and love, but that is irrelevant. Statistics are clear. Babies with extra needs rarely get adopted.

And you will never, not ever, be in foster care.

So I need a plan.

Everyone else sees this as back-pedaling. They think I'm making a plan in case I back out.

They are wrong.

I am making a plan in case they back out. In case the warm, loving home I choose for you vanishes, like so many others in the forums.

I am not naive enough to believe bad things could never happen to me.

If a family backs out of this adoption plan, it will be because you have a severe medical issue.

If I keep you, then I will need an ultra-fast career with decent pay and benefits.

If I keep you, I will need skills.

I ignore the voice in my head that knows if I can't handle a healthy child on my own, why do I think I am equipped for a more demanding setup?

I silence the voice. I am ill-equipped for all of it. I know that.

But I am better equipped than the state.

At least I have love.

I enroll in every nursing course I can at the local tech school.

If I had to, I could whip this into full-time work with health insurance within a year.

I hope I don't have to.

33

ENTWINED

Mom has a friend who has adopted two sons. She tells him about me.

He brings her a CD: Patty Kakac and the Pinetones. "A gift for your daughter," he tells her.

I listen to a single track, on repeat, until I know every word and every note.

Love of Letting Go

The day you placed her in my arms

Our lives became entwined.

The daughter that you carried

From that moment, became mine.

You said Congratulations,

now you're her mom and dad.

I never knew how so much joy,

could be mixed with so much sad.

But you needed to fly

And try and find the place where you belong.

Life gets hard and lonely.

Remember you are strong.

Sometimes the greatest love to give

Is the love of letting go

And you were wise enough to know.

You were wise enough to know.

Tears filled your eyes

when it came time to part.

You wanted so to hold your child,

close to your heart.

But you knew she needed so much more

than you could ever give.

Takes more than dreams and fantasies

for a growing child to live.

But you needed to fly…

Now this child means so much to me,

so much more than I can say

But you will always be with her

in a very special way

For you gave to her a lesson

it takes years for most to know

That sometimes the greatest love of all

Is the love of letting go.

I search for more adoption music and find a full playlist of songs that I will pull out every year around April, when thoughts of you push everything else away and I need to sink into the emotion of you. Somehow, it feels less alone when the music understands.

34

BRYAN

"We were talking with Joyce at the wedding, and they said you're still looking for parents."

Pause.

"I am."

"Well, we're wondering if you would consider us."

I am stunned. I had no idea they would be interested.

I picture the cousin Bryan of my childhood, white-blond hair and farm-tanned skin, crawling through the hayloft looking for kittens. I don't really know him as an adult.

I picture his wife Angela at the last family wedding, dancing with toddlers, her focus tracking the kids everywhere, bending low to listen to a request and fill a cup of punch.

. . .

I don't know my answer yet, but that's okay. I might eliminate them immediately if we want different things.

"You should know," I say, "I require three things."

"I won't put her in foster care. Apparently, it's standard for babies to go into foster care during the first few weeks, when I can still legally change my mind. I won't do that. You have to trust me not to change my mind."

"Okay," he says.

"The adoption can't be a secret. I don't want this to be something she learns about when she turns twelve. It's devastating for adoptees. She needs to know her whole life."

"Okay," he says.

The next one is the big eliminator. I take a breath.

"And I want a fully open adoption. I want to see her. Letters and pictures on how she's doing. I'm not going to try to be her mom or anything, but I want her to know me and know I'm her birthmother."

"Well, this sounds okay," he says, "but I should talk about all of this with Ang."

The perfect response.

Those requests are too big, too heavy to accept without

thought, discussion, and planning. This requires complete buy-in from everyone.

"Okay," I say.

And so we begin.

35

FORUMS VI

On the birthparents page, I see a recurring story.

"My son, who I gave up twenty-four years ago, wants to reconnect. My husband and three kids don't know anything about him. I'm afraid if I tell my husband, he will hate me for lying to him all these years. But I don't want my son to feel unwanted. I just don't know how to add him to my life without destroying it."

"No one knows I gave up a baby in high school. I'm terrified if anyone finds out, they will hate me for lying. The agency has a letter for me, but I can't go get it. I'll lose everyone I love."

"I recently reconnected with my daughter, but she thinks I am ashamed of her because I don't want to let her meet her half-siblings. I am not ashamed. I am afraid. No one knows she exists, and I don't know what will happen to my family if I tell them about her."

This post appears every day.

New authors.

New language.

But the same story.

And on the adoptee page, there's another story.

"Why doesn't my birthmother want to get to know me?"

"Why won't my birthparents respond?"

"Why is she ashamed of me?"

I won't do this.

I don't know yet how to avoid it. I have no solutions. Just resolve.

I will hold a space open for you. You will always be welcome in my world.

36

BASKETBALL

Mark is eleven. He has a game on Saturday.

He asks Mom not to go. "Dad said he might come."

At eleven years old, Mark knows that if Mom's car is in the parking lot, his dad won't go in.

Mom agrees to stay home.

Mark is excited all week. Elated.

His dad is going to watch him play. The first time ever.

No, he does not need a ride home. His dad will drive him.

At eleven, he does not know.

At seventeen, I do. Dad is not coming.

· · ·

I do not want to see our father. I have secrets of my own.

Too big, too hard to deal with right now.

Shove them down. Put them away. Just avoid seeing him.

But Mark, tenderhearted, optimistic. Waiting for Saturday. "Dad will see me make a basket."

At eleven, he knows little.

At seventeen, I know too much.

I do not want to run into my father.

I can't. Not now. I have too much to deal with right now.

But Mark, so excited, will be devastated to be left alone, the only kid with no parent to drive him home.

I decide last-minute.

At seventeen, I know. Dad will not show up.

The bleachers are hard and my belly is large. I take a court-side seat.

Mark is on the bench. He scans the crowd, finally lands on me.

Big eyes, surprised. Full smile.

I can't help but grin.

When he's in play, I watch every move. He steals. He passes. He finds me.

I clap and smile and nod and fill my gestures with every measure of support I can.

He watches my reaction, then runs off to catch up to his team.

After the game, I join the parents on the court, searching for sweaty boys to pile into minivans.

I am self-conscious. It's a small town, a rural town, a Catholic school team. I don't want to embarrass him.

He runs to me. "Did you see me steal from that really fast kid?"

"I saw! It was great!"

He looks around the court one last time. "Are you gonna drive me home?"

Embarrassment, but my belly didn't cause it. My showing up helped alleviate it. "Yup. You ready to go?"

We stop for ice cream on the way home.

37

CHOICES

Discussions with Bryan and Angela are frank. This is not a time for coyness. Everything has to be wide-open. All topics are on the table.

Circumcision for boys?

Bikinis and pierced ears for girls?

How do you feel about the title birthmother?

Do you want her to know anything about her birthfather?

What if she's a tomboy?

What if he wants to take ballet?

What if they are gay?

What if there's something wrong with the baby? Are you okay with a special needs child? Do I need a back-up plan?

Over the next few weeks, we talk about it all.

. . .

Some questions make them stumble.

It's unfair to them. No other parents have to prove their fitness to procreate. No other parents have to defend future theoretical decisions based on no information, just to be granted the honor of raising a child.

And it's not just me.

The adoption agency lady is worse.

"Did your father tell you he loved you?"

"Is your mother proud of you?"

"Do you smoke? Do you drink? How much money do you make? And how do you spend it?"

Bryan and Angela rise to the challenge.

With me, they are gentle and honest.

Yes, probably circumcision.

Yes, pierced ears, but no bikinis, probably.

Tomboys are fine. Ballet might be a struggle, but that's just because ballet is terrible.

Gay is no problem. Half my college ball team was gay. We would love a gay child just like any other.

I ask more impertinent questions.

"Will you stay home or put her in daycare?"

"How long will you stay home?"

"How many kids do you want?"

"Will she be an only child?"

I do not want her to be an only child.

They answer everything. If they are annoyed with my questions, they don't show it.

Sometimes, I ask the same questions, weeks apart, to make sure I get the same answers. They are consistent and truthful in their responses.

We discuss everything and I wonder how many more things I should have asked that I don't know to ask yet. And then I think of more.

"What if one of you dies?"

"What if you both die?"

"What if you lose your job?"

I get a lot of practice discussing taboo topics and asking inappropriate questions.

A weaker couple would have bailed.

An immature couple would have crumbled.

A more selfish couple would have clammed up, offered short patronizing answers and informally shown me that these are private issues and none of my concern.

But Bryan and Angela, tough and solid and thoughtful and honest, can see that, as long as you are part of me, it is all my concern. As they pull together to meet this crazy set of obstacles required to build their family, they show me, again and again, they are committed.

Unified.

Honest.

And loving.

What more could I ask?

I choose them.

38

AGENCY LADY I

The adoption agency lady, the woman who is supposed to represent me, support me, be my advocate, is not.

She thinks she is.

She thinks I'm just a dumb kid, too young to know what I want, too naive to make a plan.

I tell her I will never allow you to go to foster care.

"It is required," she says. "We don't place infants with adoptive parents until after the fourteen-day waiting period."

"If I'm going to trust the parents with my child for eighteen years," I say, "they need to trust me for two weeks."

"It is not standard," she says.

"I don't care," I say.

"Too many birthmothers change their minds," she says. "It is to protect the adoptive parents."

"I'm not changing my mind," I say. "It is crucial the baby has a chance to bond with the parents as quickly as possible. She will already be disoriented because they aren't me. I won't do that to her twice."

"It is against policy," she says.

"Then when I have this baby, I'm giving her to Bryan and Angela to 'babysit' until the adoption goes through. I'm sure I can find a lawyer to handle the paperwork."

"I'll see what I can do," she says.

39

FORUMS VII

I post to the birthparent forums:

"I am nine months pregnant. (I have already chosen parents. Please don't offer.) What advice do you wish someone had given you to make the next few months easier?"

I receive an outpouring of love from birthparents, adoptees, and their parents. A few birthparents offer, "Don't do it. Keep the baby." I ignore a lot of the advice, but a few pieces I cling to.

#1: No alcohol, no drugs.

This is the most common theme. You will be in pain and it's easier to numb yourself, but numbing doesn't make the pain go away. It just delays it. You still have to deal with it eventually. Grieve now, when you are surrounded with love and support.

Grief is easier to handle when it's fresh. If you sober up in three years and then try to grieve, you will find far less support. Your friends and family will have expected you to move on already. And now you'll have more regrets to deal with. All those dreams you have now, the dreams you will be free to chase because you will not be raising a child, go chase them. It is really horrifying to clean up three years later and realize your life is even more messed up than it was when you got pregnant, and you haven't even begun to work through the pain yet.

This is good advice and I plan to take it.

#2: No pregnancy, no pets.

Another common theme. You will feel like a mother. A mom without a child and a massive hole to fill. You will want to get pregnant right away. It sounds crazy, but biology is tough to ignore and everything in you will crave a baby. Don't do it. You will not be in a better position to raise a kid in six months from now than you were six months ago. Don't believe the hormones. Hormones lie.

And no pets. If you don't get pregnant, you'll want to fill the hole with three dogs, six cats, four rabbits and lizards and birds and every broken, lonely animal in need of a good home. Don't do it. If you go to college, you can't take them with you and will have to go through the loss of giving them up. If you don't go to college because you can't give up another damn thing, then you give up college and that hurts too. Just accept that there will be a massive, gaping hole that hurts like hell and don't try to fill it or numb it. Just let it hurt and move forward anyway.

This, too, is good advice. I plan to focus on school and exercise and pour my love into my sister's kid.

#3. Listen to yourself.

Write out a list of all the reasons you are giving your baby away. Do it now, before the birth hormones kick in. You are more clear-headed now. Give it to someone you trust and if you start questioning your decision, ask them to remind you why you are doing this.

Only one person recommended this, but I do it. I spend many nights in the blue light of the computer, writing a list of all that you deserve. I envision all aspects of our life together, and what it would look like for you without me. I write as clearly as I can why I need to do this.

I never waver, but that may be due, in part, to this exercise. This time spent figuring out the whole reason, the whole story.

Yes, I am young, but it's not youth alone.

Yes, I am poor, but it's not just poverty.

Yes, I am scared, but the fear is for good reason.

I add line after line, one night at a time, one vision a day, until there is nothing left to waver on.

I give a copy to your parents and a copy to Rachel.

This is a good decision, I tell myself. Then I cling to that,

through my fear,

through the grief,

and into my unknown future.

40

BELLY

I love my giant belly.

This globe, this world, this entire ecosystem I carry as part of me.

Your whole world, inside me.

At night, I lie on the couch, shirt hitched up so my bare belly is exposed.

I watch you.

You roll.

You stretch.

Your knuckles trace a line down my side. I can see the nubs of your tiny hand. The heel of your foot.

. . .

When you hiccup, my belly jumps.

A little electric blip throughout my body.

I lie and watch you and am amazed.

My belly, your whole world.

My whole world, inside this belly.

41

SHOPPING

Mom and I are shopping for pajamas that fit over my belly.

Aunt Eileen, Mom's sister, is shopping too. For her first grandbaby.

Angela is with her, shopping for the nursery.

In a flash, my heart cracks a little.

"Do you want to come with us?" Angela asks.

Yes! Yes I want to! "Are you sure?" I ask.

"Of course." Angela is nervous-excited-uncomfortable. It's visible in her walk, her attention, her quiet comments. She is skeptical. Until you are born, you are not hers, and preparing for you could just be setting herself up for an empty nursery and broken heart.

. . .

I join Eileen and Angela, up and down the baby aisles.

Crib sheets, bottles, toys. Eileen encourages Angela to make selections, get ready.

Angela buys one package of diapers. Her fear is visible in her empty cart.

I watch Angela.

I catch her watching me.

I wish I didn't need her, didn't need her to raise this child.

My guess is she wishes she didn't need me, didn't need me to grow this child.

But we need each other, and we both know it.

The whole situation is strange.

My first glimpse at my next few years, where Angela and I are on guard, trying to show our best selves, both hurt and happy to be in this moment together.

This will become a familiar sensation:

The wound and the salve occur simultaneously.

42

AGENCY LADY II

The adoption agency lady is supposed to help me make a birth plan.

I tell her my birth plan. "When I go into labor, I will call Bryan and Angela. Only Rachel will be in the room during delivery, but after it's all over, I'll invite Bryan and Angela in to meet her."

"No," she says. "It is better if they meet her privately in the nursery."

"No," I say. "They will meet her in my room after I deliver."

She shakes her head sadly. "It will be too hard for you. You don't understand how these hormones will affect you. You will want to change your mind. We will move Baby to the nursery and introduce the adoptive parents there."

. . .

I speak slowly, as if to a disobedient three-year-old. "I will hand her directly to Angela. In my hospital room. And I will be there."

The adoption agency lady and I have fought over nearly every point of my plan. She is finally starting to recognize this stubborn face, this determined voice. She gives in.

43

FORUMS VIII

Adoptees hate having multiple names.

Identity, they say. It's hard to know if they are more Justin or Brock, more Penelope or Brooke. The day they first learn the old name, the real name, the past name, they don't know how to work the information into a new identity.

This, at least, I have the power to avoid.

I call Bryan. "I don't want the baby to have two names. Tell me what you plan to name him or her, and that is what I will write on the birth certificate."

For the next few weeks, I hope they pick something good.

When we speak next, Bryan and Angela present me with a gift, a better idea, an offer that sets the tone for our future inter-actions.

"We have three names for each gender and we'd like you to decide."

And with that, we have order.

In all things, your needs come first.

They determine what is best for you, and they are kind enough to allow me to participate.

44

PULSE

My heart beats wildly out of control.

My face is flushed.

I am scared.

I can feel my pulse in my wrists, my neck, my chest, my forehead.

I Google, "heart racing pregnant."

Is this a symptom of labor I don't know about?

Or is something wrong with my baby?

I call my doctor. She fits me in right away. I leave the clinic with a heart rate monitor and a referral for a cardiologist appointment the next day.

The cardiologist sends me home with pills and instructions: If my heart races like this again, don't wait to see him. Go directly to the emergency room.

45

AGENCY LADY III

The adoption agency lady tries to convince me it would be best if, after having the baby, I send you to a foster home right away, the first night, and I move out of the maternity ward. Heal in some other hospital wing.

She is wrong.

"As long as I am in the hospital, I want her there, too."

A little selfish, maybe, but I believe you and I will both do better with a little bit of transition time.

Hello to goodbye in three days.

I make two selfish decisions.

. . .

1. I will not breastfeed you.

If I do, I fear that whenever my breasts fill and leak and ache with the lack of you, I will fear you are hungry and alone and ache with the lack of me. I do not want to punish my psyche this way.

2. I send you to the nursery to sleep at night.

If you stay in my room, I will grow accustomed to the sound of your sleep, the smell of your skin, your presence beside me. At home, when I wake at night, I will think it is you, far away, in distress, and there will be nothing I can do about it. I do not want to torture my heart this way.

46

PLAN

I have planned for you.

Rachel will help me through labor.

Bryan and Ang will meet you at the hospital the day you are born.

Bryan and Ang will love you, raise you, and be amazing parents to you.

I will be as present and involved as they allow me to be.

I have thought through so many details of your plan. Where you will be every moment until your adoption is finalized. How many visits, letters, and pictures will be exchanged later.

I know your plan.

And then, I start to plan for me.

I can't stay here. I'll need to leave. My heart can't take it here, sleeping on the couch where my giant belly used to hiccup, moving through the halls my big belly used to bump. I can't stay here without you.

I need somewhere to go for the summer.

In the fall, I'll go back to St. Cloud State, live in the dorms. Pick up where I left off.

And I plan to heal.

I start looking into grief. I read C.S. Lewis. I read self-help. I read psychology papers on the peculiar kind of grief associated with losing children. Mom shares some resources she received from her divorced women's group. I save writings, lists of recommended books, and I do my best to prepare myself for a loss that is going to hurt like hell.

47

MICE

I wake up to screaming.

It is Rachel, on the loveseat next to me, screaming and thrashing in her blankets. "Get them off! Get them off!"

Before I register what is happening, Mom launches herself out of bed and to the living room. But she forgets her bedroom door is closed and smacks her head into the door.

"It's a dream." I shake Rachel. "You're dreaming. Wake up."

Mom comes out to the living room, one hand on her quickly bruising forehead, and flips on the light. "What is it?" She looks directly at me. "Are you hurt?"

"It's Rachel. She was dreaming."

Rachel is awake now, still flushed red, but calming down. She notices Mom's head. "What happened to you?"

"She ran into her bedroom door," I laugh.

Rachel laughs, too. "Why?"

I smack her. "Because you were screaming and she thought someone was hurt!"

We are all laughing. Mom digs in the freezer for ice.

"What's going on?" Marks asks, still half asleep.

"There were mice crawling on me," Rachel says. "They were everywhere."

"No more falling asleep to Cinderella," I laugh. "Apparently, it's traumatic for you."

No one can go back to sleep now.

We stay up, watching mice-free Disney movies and eating ice cream, Mom with an ice pack on her forehead.

48

GIFT

I prepare for you. Prepare to say goodbye to you.

I shop for a gift, something I can send with you. What could possibly be good enough? Could mean enough? Could say enough?

Mom and I wander the aisles. She touches every soft blanket, every onesie with a big-eyed animal. Her longing to buy for you, to nest for your arrival, is visible in her every motion.

She resists. You will not be her grandbaby to spoil. She will have to step back and allow her sister that role.

Eventually, I buy a small, painted toy-box-style trunk.

To it, I add the softest lamb. A blanket.

I consider adding the jumper with the flower on the belly. I still have not told anyone it exists. I'm not sure why, but I don't want to let it go. It stays hidden.

The best gift I can think to give you is a reason, an explanation, a very clear message that this is me loving you the best way I know how. I add a printed copy of all the things I wish for you.

49

MY WISH FOR YOU

I could keep you. It would be possible, hard, but possible, to take care of you.

But you deserve more than that.

If I keep you, our life will be unstable.

I don't have a good job, and I can't get one. I have no education, skills, or network. We will be broke.

You deserve a home.

With me, you will live in a government-subsidized apartment with a busy street out front and an alley in back.

I want your childhood memories to be of home, the smell of

the carpet when you lie on the floor watching TV, the feeling of the banister when you slide down the stairs. You deserve a backyard with a sandbox and trees to climb.

You deserve consistency.

You deserve to grow up in a single school.

With me, you will move from home to home, jumping daycares and school districts. You will have to leave your friends, leave your community, over and over until I am on my feet with a stable job to support us both.

You deserve medical insurance.

With me, I cannot take you to the doctor without debating whether you are sick enough to warrant not paying rent. I will be forced to wait too long, skip too many visits.

When you need glasses, you deserve two pairs, so you can break one without worry.

With me, you will have a life of duct tape and hot glue.

You deserve the best daycare.

With me, you will have the most affordable.

. . .

You deserve a carefree childhood, filled with scraped knees and small problems. You should cry when your ice cream melts or you lose a toy.

With me, you will know in your bones the stress of day-to-day survival, waiting for welfare checks, trying to fill empty cupboards and gas tanks.

You deserve time.

A mother who can care for you when you're sick, play with you when you're well.

With me, I will be too tired after long shifts, long bus rides, long stressful days without anyone to help carry the load. With me, you will come home to an empty house after school. You will lie in the nurse's office when you're sick because I won't be able to leave work and there is no one else to help.

You deserve to thrive, to be given the best chance to succeed at whatever you love.

With me, you will be the kid in school who gets made fun of because your homework is never done because I had to work late. You will be the kid who can't read as quickly as the others because no one will have time to read to you when you're little.

You will have no science fair project. You will join no clubs, participate in no sports. Too expensive. Too many rides will be needed. It will be too much.

You deserve a father.

A stable father who won't come and go throughout your life. You deserve a father who makes promises, and then keeps them.

You deserve someone who will rock and cradle you, hug you, teach you to build a fort in the woods. You need a role model, who will teach you how to treat others, how to treat yourself.

With me, you will see the ups and downs of my dating life. If it doesn't work out with someone, you should not feel like you lost a father. You should not feel it is your fault. But you will.

With me, you will follow my lead, learn from me how to date, how to treat yourself, how to let people treat you. I do not want you to learn these lessons from me. And I don't know how to teach you anything else.

With me, you will be the twenty-year-old who marries a man twice your age because you're looking for a father figure.

You deserve brothers and sisters.

You deserve a dog who can sleep in your bed and a clean lake to jump into in the summer. You deserve to know how it feels to dance on your father's toes, plant a garden in your own yard, go outside, and play without worry.

You deserve a home where love is constant, hugging is commonplace, and respect is inherent.

I have only seen glimpses of this world. I have no idea how to build a life like that.

You deserve to know a home, a stable happy home.

You deserve more than a life with me.

50

FORUMS IX

On the forums, I post my list of reasons I am giving you up, all that you deserve. The adoptees have so many questions, I'm hoping my words may answer some for them.

I receive an outpouring of love. Every day for a week, I read new responses.

"You expressed everything I felt for my own daughter when I placed her (DOB 11-26-1984). I have often thought of typing out the letter I wrote to her and asking to have the agency place it in her 'file' as they called it. If I thought I could type it without soaking my keyboard and shorting out my computer, I would do it! I hope all adoptees can feel encouraged and loved knowing that their bmoms, in most cases, feel the same way."

"I am going to print this out and show it to my birthmother.

We were reunited for the first time about a month ago, and I have a feeling that your posting will sit just right with how she feels about giving me up for adoption."

"Our birthmother chose adoption for all the same reasons you listed and the primary factor was that of having a loving father. Your words touched my heart. They also remind me of how much trust our birthmothers put in us adoptive parents. I for one will do my very best not to let you down in any way!"

"I'm printing this for my two little adopted daughters. We work so hard every day to give them the blessings you have described and we love them in a way that pretty much defies description. But then again, maybe it doesn't. You already know that love, don't you? As a birthmother you have the same love in your heart that we have in ours. We don't need words. Hold your head up high as you work to build your life from here on."

"I don't know why I felt so compelled to write to you. Your words just make so much sense. I always assumed that my birthmom couldn't care for me, but I never even thought about her wanting more for *me*. I always assumed it was about what was better for *her*."

"I made the same decision at your age and I have never regretted it for one second. It has been 19 years now. Please stay strong and committed to your choice. As both an adoptee and a birthmom, I understand what a complete and total act of love adoption is. You have my very best wishes."

Hundreds of people respond in a few days. I bundle their responses and print them out, add them to my hospital bag. Just in case I need to be reminded.

51

PAINT

I take mostly nursing classes at the tech school, but to get my new school district to pay for the credits, I must take one high school class.

The art teacher allows me to create an "Independent Study in Painting" course. For two hours every Monday, Wednesday, and Friday, I paint.

Quiet and alone at my table at the back of the art room.

My classmates grow younger as spring nears.

It is difficult to leave thoughts of you behind when you are a part of me, visible and visceral.

I paint Dumbo, the scene where the mother rocks him, her trunk through the metal bars. The mother locked in her cage, unable to care for her baby.

The song plays in my head.

Baby mine, don't you cry.

I paint Tarzan, the scene where he holds his palm up to his mother's, looking for connection, for sameness.

The lyrics and melody spin.

You'll be in my heart.

The other students are kind to me. Friendly even.

But I am out of sync with them.

I listen to my peers, giddy with prom plans, hookups, and break-ups.

While I plan your life and mine.

Drama and backstabbing and high school squabbling fill the room.

While I think through how to grieve this, how to move forward.

I stay silent and age quietly, singularly, during those final weeks of high school.

52

HEART

I have been taking pills for my heart for the last month and they seem to be working.

Until today.

I check my pulse. Fast, way too fast.

I try to slow my breathing. Try to calm myself.

Which scares me more, which speeds my already racing heart.

I check my pulse again. Faster, spinning out of control, far too fast.

I am due anytime now. If you come today, you will be okay.

But that also terrifies me.

I'm not ready to give birth. I don't know how to give birth.

But more important, I'm not ready to say goodbye. I need more time.

I check my pulse again. Faster, faster, speeding off the rails, can't-breathe fast.

I call the clinic. "My pulse is 140 beats per minute."

The nurse on the line disagrees with me. Clearly I took it wrong.

I call my nurse aunt who lives down the road. She swings by and takes my pulse. "151 beats per minute," she says. "You need to go in right now."

Mom packs a bag for me.

I sit on a dining room chair and focus on breathing slowly and not being scared.

It doesn't work.

Mom drives me to the hospital. I am checked in right away. Not into maternity, and for that, I am grateful.

The doctor checks my pulse, listens to the baby's heartbeat.

"Baby is fine," she says.

I get an IV and within minutes my heart calms, my panic lessens.

. . .

Mom sits next to me, stiff and afraid. She won't leave my side.

"Mark is probably getting off the bus soon," I say.

She doesn't want to leave me here alone.

"I'm fine," I say. "Go pick him up. I'm fine."

Nurses come and go. They ask how far along I am. They ask about pain, about contractions.

"Only Braxton-Hicks," I say.

I feel better now. I feel safe, taken care of, my IV drip keeps that blip-blip-blip on the monitor in a sane, consistent rhythm.

Nurses listen to my heartbeat, listen to yours. You are fine. Only I am a mess.

I look younger than I am and my scared eyes can't help.

One nurse is blatantly rude to me. Another is extra kind and asks me about my plan. "What grade are you in?"

"I'm a senior, but I take all my classes at the tech school."

"Do you plan to breastfeed?"

"No."

"Do you have a nursery set up?"

"I'm giving her up for adoption," I say.

. . .

The rude nurse pauses in her work for a minute, looks at me, then walks out.

The kind one stays and asks more questions.

I have read horror stories on the forums, well-meaning nurses who refuse to bring babies to birthmothers, thinking them hormone-rattled and too weak to stick to the adoption plan if given the chance to hold their babies. Nurses who take away the birthmothers' right to say goodbye.

I recognize this opportunity and make my requests very clear.

"It will be an open adoption. Her parents will be here when I deliver. I'm keeping the baby with me while I'm in the hospital, but then she'll go home with her parents. I plan to hold her, see her, and spend time with her during those couple of days."

"I also plan to let her parents see her as much as they want while they're here. If there are any new parent training sessions or that kind of thing, we will all go."

This nurse has soft eyes. "Won't that be hard?"

"Everything about this is hard," I say. "I'm doing it anyway."

The gossip spreads through the nurses, and the mood shifts. For the two days it takes to settle my heart, I am doted on.

They play Disney movies for me over the closed-circuit TV.

They bring me extra dessert, extra blankets. They tiptoe in at night to check on me and try not to wake me too much when taking my vitals.

I am swaddled in compassion from these women and, for once, I am thankful for those forum horror stories that prompted me to speak up. The entire staff knows me, knows our plan.

And when, two weeks later, I return in labor, I am not challenged. I am heard.

I find compassionate nurses ready to help me execute the plan I have spent months figuring out.

No one interferes. Everyone helps.

And I am so grateful for my wild racing heart.

53

MUCUS PLUG

I am overdue. My back hurts. I am uncomfortable in every way.

But I don't mind too much. I practically starved this baby in the early months. If you need a few extra days to catch up, you can have them. I'm not ready to say goodbye yet anyway.

I go in for another checkup. Once a week, now that my due date has come and gone.

The doctor stretches a tape measure from my bust line to my pelvic line and captures the measurement of my enormous belly hump. "She's gained about two pounds in these last couple weeks. How are the contractions?"

"Braxton-Hicks contractions every day now," I say.

. . .

She checks for dilation. "Nothing yet, but you've lost your mucus plug. I'm guessing we'll see this baby in the next few days."

The idea makes my heart spin. I nod.

Rachel calls from the salon. "How'd it go?"

"I lost my mucus plug," I say.

"You did?" I can hear her turn away from the phone and shout excitedly, "Alycea lost her mucus plug!" A gaggle of stylists in the background gets excited with her.

"God! Why did you have to tell everyone that? Gross."

"Do I need to come home?" she asks. "Is it happening today?"

"No. It's fine."

"Call me if anything changes."

54

TODAY

A week later, I am stabbed awake at 1:00 a.m.

My back is being knifed. It takes a moment to recognize it is happening from the inside.

They talked about this in the birthing classes I went to with Rachel. Sometimes labor feels like back pain.

I watch the clock as I am shanked repeatedly. Then, I lean over from the couch and tap Rachel, sound asleep on the love seat, her feet hanging over the edge.

"Hey. My back hurts."

"Do you need something?" she asks.

"I think I'm in labor."

She sits up. "You are?" In her voice, excitement. Fear. "Are you okay? Do you need to go in?"

"No, I'm okay, I think." My back twinges again and I can't speak for a minute. I scrunch my face. When the pain loosens, I let out a breath. "I've been watching the clock. It's not often, every twenty or thirty minutes. I'm not even sure these are contractions."

"Should we wake up Mom? What do you want to do?"

"I don't know."

"Let's call the nurse hotline and ask," Mom says after Rachel wakes her up.

Mom calls. "Yes, she's two weeks overdue. No, there's no spotting. No, her water hasn't broken, but the doctor said at the last check up that she lost her mucus plug."

"Mom!" Why does everyone insist on talking about my mucus plug?

"Yes, she has an appointment with the doctor at nine. Okay, thank you."

"Since you have an appointment today anyway," Mom says, "they said stay home and try to get some rest until then. It's probably more Braxton Hicks, but it could be real labor. Unless something changes, though, we should just wait for your appointment."

Our collective anxiety and not-very-hushed voices have woken Mark. "What's going on?" he asks, his face sleepy.

"I'm might have the baby today," I say.

55

DISTRACTION

The doctor confirms it. Labor has started.

"This is a good slow start. Go home. Let it progress naturally. And come back when your contractions are five to ten minutes apart."

Jitters.

But also, I am ready.

I know the hospital now.

I know the staff.

I know the plan.

And my back is killing me and I'd really like that to stop.

I call Rachel at work and she heads home immediately.

Mom calls her sister, who calls Bryan and Ang. They live three hours away. They will both leave work and start driving.

Mom has a migraine. It is ninety degrees and she is hot and miserable. She can't take the light or the noise of the house, so she lies down in her bedroom in the dark.

And then we wait.

But waiting is boring and nerve-wracking.

I check and double-check my hospital bag.

Everything is ready.

And we keep waiting, in the quiet.

No TV. No noise to aggravate Mom's migraine.

"I can't sit here anymore," I say.

"What do you want to do?" Rachel asks.

"I don't want to hang around the hospital all day. Want to go shopping? Get moving? That should speed things along a bit, if I'm on my feet."

We call Aunt Eileen and ask if she wants to join us. She is excited by the invite, excited to be a part of the event.

Her first grandbaby.

Main Street in this tiny town has three stores worth wandering through, and we've been through them many times before. But we walk through them again, look at everything, touch everything.

Contractions are strengthening, and I have to stop walking, hold onto a handrail and breathe through them. Then we resume our slow meandering around town.

Another contraction, and a woman frantically tries to find a chair for me so I can sit down.

I shake my head and wave her away. When the contraction ends, I thank her. "But this is the point, this is why we're here. To get things rolling."

At noon, my contractions are about eight minutes apart. My water hasn't broken. But, we've examined every store in town, my back hurts, my feet are tired, and I can't go home to the silent dark house.

"You want to go to the hospital?" Rachel asks.

"Sure."

56

HOSPITAL

I get the new delivery suite, never before used. When we did the hospital tour with the birthing class, it was still under construction. It has a large tub and wide open spaces.

A nurse suggests a bath may speed things along.

I maneuver into the tub, choosing my timing carefully. Start right after one contraction ends and settle in before the next one starts.

Rachel feeds me Jelly Bellies and I try to guess the flavors.

"Pear, my favorite. Blech. Popcorn."

I get out of the bath and try walking the halls. Try lying down. Try sitting.

. . .

Three hours later, there's been little progress.

Rachel massages my hands and feet with lotion, pampering techniques she uses at the salon sometimes. She keeps me calm and laughing between the contractions.

"The baby's heart rate is even, consistent," a nurse says. "She doesn't seem to be in any distress, so we'll just let things continue."

This nurse is hugely pregnant. She was not here the weekend I had heart troubles, but I like her. She has a calm way about her.

When Mark gets home from school, he and Mom come to the hospital. Mom slips into my room. The pain in her head is almost visible, radiating off her with every blip of the heart monitor and glare of the lights.

"Since Mom is here, do you mind if I go smoke?" Rachel asks.

"No, that's fine. Go ahead."

She races out the door.

Mom is helpful, right up until she witnesses that first contraction.

I do what I've been doing all day. Stop talking, scrunch my face up, and breathe breathe breathe.

Mom flutters around, nervous scared energy, unable to watch me in pain without doing something to help.

"Should I call someone? Get you water? Do you need a pillow? Do you need drugs? Have you had drugs? Ice chips?"

With every contraction, she tenses, feeling my pain as her own, until my breathing normalizes, the pain fades.

"This is how it's supposed to go, Mom. I'm okay."

She is visibly not okay.

"You know, I'm doing all right. You can go back out with Mark. I'll be fine."

"Oh, I couldn't leave you alone. No, I won't leave."

She doesn't leave, and the second contraction spurs another round of empathetic pain and rattled movements to add to her migraine.

When Rachel comes back, Mom disappears to the waiting room, where Mark, Eileen, Bryan, and Ang all wait.

"I hope you enjoyed that," I say. "Because you don't get to leave again until this is over."

57

SLEEP

At five, they call the doctor in. She thinks breaking the water will help.

It does.

Contractions are doubly painful and start coming more closely together. I opt for my shot of drugs now, the spinal block that will ease me through this.

Instantly, I feel nothing.

No pain. No contractions. Nothing.

It is the most amazing feeling.

The doctor keeps a hand on my belly for the next few minutes. The monitor shows a contraction rise and fall in intensity, but I can't feel a thing.

. . .

"Everything is progressing well now," the doctor says. "I'll check back on you in about an hour."

For forty-five glorious minutes, I sleep. I haven't slept since the back pains woke me in the middle of the night, and I am exhausted. Sleep. Wonderful sleep.

58

BABY

The doctor wakes me. "You're ready to push," she says.

The nurses help me sit in a better position.

Rachel is nervous. She keeps patting my hand like a dog. I don't stop her.

"I'm going to throw up," I say.

The pregnant nurse appears with a basin, and I spit vomit. Seems oddly fitting given how you and I started this pregnancy.

Rachel holds a water cup for me to sip.

And then, with my next contraction, we begin.

I push and throw up, alternating between the two, every few minutes. We try different positions. Things get more painful, pain I thankfully can no longer remember. That drug-induced bliss is completely gone.

I scream and throw up and push and cry.

. . .

Four and a half hours later, you arrive.

"Do you want to cut the umbilical cord?" the doctor asks me.

She hands me scissors. I steady my shaking hands.

I release you from me.

She places you on my chest, red and wrinkled and angry.

You are incredible.

Full head of dark hair.

Tiny little wrinkled arms, fists clenched tight.

A baby. A living, breathing baby.

You, who I have known for so many months, finally made visible. Finally real.

I could feel you.

I could always feel you.

But now to see you, to hold you, to have you with me in this world.

You belong here. And the world feels somehow more balanced.

"Hello," I say.

I stare at you until Rachel interrupts. "Oh my God, the placenta is huge!"

59

TWENTY

For twenty minutes, you are mine.

You have been washed, weighed, and evaluated. You are perfectly healthy.

Rachel tells everyone in the waiting room that you have arrived and we are doing well.

The nurses clean up the room. The doctor fills out a chart.

And you and I, for twenty minutes, lie in that bed together.

Your big eyes.

Your weird cone-shaped head.

Your tight fists.

Skin so soft it feels make-believe.

. . .

Nobody rushes me.

Nobody takes you away.

You and I have a few moments to just be together.

"I'm ready," I tell Rachel when she returns from her well-earned break. "Let's introduce her to Bryan and Ang."

60

INTRODUCTION

A soft knock on the partially opened door.

Your mom's head, cautious, making sure she is allowed in.

Your dad, inching behind her.

Their eyes find you immediately, then look to me.

I had practiced saying so many things at this moment.

"Meet your daughter."

"Katarina, meet your parents."

"This is your mom."

I don't know what I end up saying.

Your mom reaches for you, slowly.

She does not pick you up. She does not take you away from me.

She waits for me to place you in her arms.

I cannot imagine how hard it was for her to wait like that.

She cradles you, brushes your cheek with a fingertip.

Bryan leans close and for a moment, the three of you look like a painting, an emotion caught in space.

61

NURSE

I am moved from the delivery suite to a maternity room down the hall.

The pregnant nurse helps me out of bed. Helps me change into a clean robe. She gathers my bag and all my things, pushes my wheelchair, and settles me into my new bed. She tucks the blankets up around me. Asks if I need anything.

"You must be exhausted," I say. "You've been by my side since I showed up almost twelve hours ago."

She nods.

"Is your shift over soon?" I ask.

She smiles at me. "My shift was over a couple hours ago. The nurses told me about you. About your plan." She pushes a fist into her lower back and stretches. "I didn't want to leave you. I wanted to make sure you would be okay."

62

ETIQUETTE II

I give birth to a healthy baby girl.

People love and support me.

How are they supposed to show it?

I receive flowers at the hospital.

A garden of flowers. The florist tags read:

"To Alycea. Love, the Johnsons." This short sentiment is perfect.

Some people buy cards. Many cards are blank, with awkward scrawled messages.

I receive a handful of supportive cards.

"I'm here to support you in any way I can."

I receive carefully chosen words.

"You are brave and loving and will get through this."

A few like this:

"My sympathy during this difficult time."

From your parents, a beautiful letter, the perfect message, that makes me cry.

And one.

Just one.

From my little brother. Eleven and innocent. Oblivious to the social requirements.

He picked it out himself and is excited for me to open it.

"Congratulations on your baby girl."

His is my favorite.

63

VISITORS

We have an endless stream of visitors in the hospital.

Joyce brings Desiree, three years old with red pigtails and big eyes. Joyce holds you and invites Desiree to look.

Desiree leans close and unwraps your blanket, pulls off your tiny pink sock. She wants to see your toes. She pokes them.

Joyce covers your feet, wraps you snuggly.

Desiree complains until Joyce lets her unwrap your blanket and free your toes.

You don't seem to mind.

My older brother fits a quick trip into the middle of a college class week to see us. Aunts, uncles, cousins all appear.

. . .

The past four months, living in this town where my mom grew up, building relationships with her family, the family that was always there, but I was not connected to before. Not like this.

These four months pulled me into a circle of kin like I didn't know was possible.

Angela's parents, sisters, brother,

All of whom I have never met before.

Mom's friends, the ones who still come around after her divorce, the ones who still show up for her.

One old friend of mine from high school. Just one.

Her presence surprises me and for a moment I look back at all the other tough moments in my childhood and see how many times this one girl has appeared beside me. I wonder how I never saw that before.

I am amazed at how many visitors we have, me and Katarina and Bryan and Ang.

For all those nights of feeling alone, I am not alone now.

64

HELLO. GOODBYE.

You stay in the hospital with me. Bryan and Ang and visitors come and go.

In the evenings, it is the four of us. Bryan. Ang. You. Me.

We all take turns feeding you bottles.

We watch reruns of Frasier and Friends. We focus on you and comment on your every move.

Looks like she spit up a little.

Do you think she's hungry?

She has her eyes open. Look how she watches you.

We talk about the weather, about the commercials.

Nothing is the right thing to talk about, and eventually, the reruns win.

The reruns feel like home. Familiar and comfortable and shared.

At night, Bryan and Ang go to Eileen's.

You sleep alone in the nursery.

Me in my room.

In this way, we spend three days.

Saying hello.

Saying goodbye.

65

AID

New parents receive first aid training at the hospital. There are multiple new babies today and the instructor is scheduling a class.

I call your parents, make sure they know what time to attend. We all go to the class.

Bryan holds you as though you are glass. Every movement has him gingerly checking.

Are you warm?

Are you comfortable?

I watch Bryan watch you and my heart is full. Calm. Certain.

You will be okay.

66

BATH

A nurse arrives to teach the new parents how to give you a bath.

She offered to do it yesterday. I asked her to come back today when your parents are here.

Your mom and dad are nervous when she arrives.

There is so much tension in the room.

Careful. We are all being careful.

We are all fragile. The whole scene ready to crack on a stray comment, a disobedient hormone.

The nurse tells us we must start with your eyes, wash the cleanest parts first.

You are tightly wrapped in your blanket.

Bryan murmurs to you and uses the soft cloth dipped in a basin of warm water and wipes your eyes,

like caressing a baby bird,

or a bomb,

or some terrifying bird-bomb hybrid.

Ang is quiet.

I say not a word.

We are all so careful.

The nurse adds energy and words, pulls the focus to her, and we are permitted to breathe again.

67

ALONE

You and I are alone.

Bryan and Ang have left for the evening. Home to Eileen's for a nervous night's sleep before they return in the morning.

Tomorrow is leaving day. Tomorrow, they will take you. Tomorrow, I will go home without you.

You are content in my arms. You look into my eyes, awake, alert, learning me.

I examine every feature, the line in your forehead, your little pout, red cheeks.

And I suddenly realize I will never bathe you,

never change your diaper,

never dress you in clean, warm pajamas.

The certainty of this breaks me.

. . .

We are alone.

Let's do it now.

I fill a basin with warm water and find a silky soft rag. I bathe you, roll by roll.

You are clean, but I bathe you anyway.

Your eyes watch my every move. You make no noise.

I tuck you into a fresh diaper. I find a white onesie and button it around your fat legs, guide your tight fists through the arms.

I gently fold you into striped pajamas, the kind with the attached booties and mittens that keep you from scratching yourself in your sleep.

Your eyes follow me.

I lay out a blanket and wrap you in it. I don't know how to do it right, that swaddle that pins you close, but I do my best.

We curl back into bed, you propped against my side.

I try to stay awake, try to savor every last moment we have together.

I know with devastating certainty I will never have a night like this with you again.

68

MIDNIGHT

I must have dozed off. I wake in the dark, you snuggled into my side.

Tomorrow I will leave the hospital.

No longer a mother,

downgraded to birthmother,

My chapter with you over.

Tomorrow, you will go home with your parents,

No longer hopeful or expecting,

but having and holding,

To have and to hold,

you will be loved.

· · ·

I fight sleep.

You do not. You doze next to me, breathing slowly. Tiny baby breaths, safe in my arms.

One last night.

I sing to you. Every lullaby I know.

The playground songs.

The love songs.

Then finally, one melody I cannot shake.

"Save tonight. Fight the break of dawn. Come tomorrow, tomorrow you'll be gone."

I sing through tears, then through sobs.

Sometime around dawn, I fall asleep crying with you still in my arms.

69

LEAVING YOU

I get into the backseat of Mom's car.

Mom turns over the ignition, Aunt Eileen, a passenger beside her.

Her sister, now a grandma for the first time.

My mother, no longer allowed to be Grandma to this one.

I kept it together at the hospital.

I took photos with Bryan and Ang and you.

There were a few tears, but no theatrics.

Best behavior. Your parents can close the door on me any day, for any reason. I will carry that fear inside me for the next eighteen years.

But now, in the back seat, my reserves are empty.

I cry.

I take deep rattling breaths, hack out painful sobs.

Every breath hurts my stitches and the pain feels right, accurate, real.

I sob loud sobs until two words emerge stronger than the tears.

"My baby."

"My baby."

"My baby."

Mom drives on, crying silently to herself.

Her sister sits quietly, her own tears falling.

We all know there is no comfort to be found. There are no words to ease this. There is nothing to do but ache.

70

PAPERS

Seventy-two hours after you are born, I can officially sign the adoption papers. I want to do this as soon as possible. I do not want your parents withholding one ounce of love from you, for fear they might lose you. I want you to settle into your new family.

We plan to sign papers first thing Monday morning.

The night before the signing, I confirm that Derek can make it.

I will not risk signing my papers unless he has already signed his. I want no loopholes, no question marks.

The adoption lady had a hard time getting him to respond to her calls, but he answers mine.

He doesn't think he can make it. He doesn't have the gas money.

"I'll pay for your gas," I tell him. I borrow forty dollars from Mom.

He arrives early, his hair bright green today. We drive together to the bank where we have an appointment with the notary. Derek does not ease over the railroad tracks like Mom does, and the bumps hurt my stitches.

Mom and Eileen are already at the bank when we arrive.

Derek and I sign our baby away.

It takes less than ten minutes.

After, he asks, "Do you want to go get lunch or something?"

I want to curl up and die. Lie down and give in and let the earth claim me. Dissolve into the ground, a shell of a woman, nothing left but blood and bones and too much milk in swollen aching breasts. "I want to go home."

I leave with Mom. I cry the whole way home.

She drives slowly over the railroad tracks, careful not to add to my pain.

71

SHOW UP

The days following your birth teach me an unexpected lesson.

I learn that the people who show up are not always the ones I expect.

Old acquaintances take the time to drop a card in the mail because they heard I was giving a baby away, and they know it will be hard, and they want to acknowledge that I am going through something difficult right now.

Old friends who have suffered losses, suffered pain, often that I knew nothing of, will not let anyone go through that alone. People who reach out, just in case they might be exactly the person I need to talk to, to let me know that I am welcome to call anytime.

I learn that the people who love me, who support, who care for me, they say some really hurtful things.

Not on purpose, but out of love, awkwardness, and inexperience.

We do not teach people how to be around sadness, what to say around grief.

"I'm so glad you gave your baby to real parents. Now you can focus on you."

I am a real parent. And I am a damned good one, because I broke my own heart to give her everything she needed.

"She looks so much like them, people will think she's their real daughter. No one will ever have to know."

She is not a shameful secret.

This adoption is not a secret.

She is their real daughter.

And I want her to know.

"Not everyone is supposed to be a mother. God has a way of making it work out."

I never stopped being a mother. And I might still be one in the future.

"I hope these consequences help you stay on God's path in the future."

By "these consequences," are you referring to this beautiful child who I love with all my heart, who is beloved by her new family and a circle of friends and family waiting to embrace her into the community?

"Everything happens for a reason."

Why would you ever say this to a person?

Who is comforted by this trope?

Others say awkward things, not necessarily helpful, but not bad either.

"I bet you're relieved to be out of maternity clothes."

"Do you think you will tell people at college about all this?"

I learn something that I will carry with me:

The people who love me show up.

They may not know what to say, but they show up.

They may say exactly the wrong thing, but only because they bothered to appear by my side to show me they care.

I learn to look through the words. Past the words. Past the awkward and often hurtful small talk.

And see only that these are the people who show up for me.

. . .

They are easy to spot, because most people stay far, far away from situations like this.

Unpleasant. Difficult. And, depending on your lens, off-color.

Most people disappeared while I was pregnant.

A few try to reappear now that, by all visible signs, it is over.

I no longer have room for them.

My life is full.

Full of people who show up.

72

NIGHTMARE

I have a recurring nightmare.

I am shopping at Target. You have been kidnapped, but no one told me. I cross paths with your kidnapper at Target. You are crying, but I do not recognize it as your cry, because I don't know your cry.

I do not know the sound of your cry.

The idea haunts me. I can't shake it.

I sit in Biology class and obsess. I do not know the sound of your cry.

I sit in Computer Tech class and stifle tears. I cannot recognize my own baby's cry.

This is a sensitive time, just a few days after leaving the hospital. I am awash in hormones. You are with your new parents.

. . .

I've heard from Mom who heard from Eileen who heard from your dad that you are colicky. You cry all the time. You never stop.

If I call your parents, I might hear you cry.

I call. I make up a lie, something about my high school graduation party. A pretense.

Bryan answers.

You scream in the background. Loud, low-pitched, angry.

Full-lunged screaming.

My heart fills with the sound of you.

Bryan hears it is me.

Your screaming fades. A door closes.

He has found a quiet room to give me his full attention.

I want to tell him to go back. I don't want to talk to him. I want to hear you cry.

But that sounds weird and almost sadistic.

I deliver my lie. We make the conversation short. I have broken unspoken etiquette in calling so soon.

He sounds harried, uncomfortable, as though he has not slept.

But, until that night, until I heard you cry, neither did I.

73

END

There are three weeks left of high school after you are born.

My grades are high. I could skip all the remaining classes and still graduate, now with a year's worth of college credits.

Week one, I lie on the couch and cry.

I put cabbage leaves on my swollen breasts and ice on my stitches.

I watch sitcoms and write.

Mostly, I just cry.

Week two, I go back to class.

I cannot stand all that time, all those endless hours.

I cannot allow myself to collapse on this couch or one day I will not get up again.

. . .

Week three, I pack.

I am moving out.

Joyce and Matt are moving to a house.

A house with an extra room in the basement and they said I could move in with them again.

I must not have been too difficult to handle when I lived with them before. I tried to help out. I went to school, kept a job, contributed as much as I could toward my own food, babysat Desiree. I hadn't done too much to wear out my welcome, until I fell in love with Derek and invited my unemployed boyfriend to live on the couch of their two-bedroom apartment for weeks on end.

As soon as I graduate, I can move back in with them. I promise to get a job and invite no more boyfriends to move in.

I miss Desiree. I miss being a part of their growing little family.

And I have to get out of here, or I will sink into my grief and never escape.

I graduate on a Friday night.

Saturday morning, my car is packed.

I hug Mom, hug Rachel, hug Mark.

I crank my radio full volume and drive away.

PART II

AFTER

74

JAKE

I show up on moving day and haul boxes from Joyce and Matt's little apartment to the trucks, then from the trucks into their new house in the suburbs. This is the most I've moved in weeks. The exercise feels good.

And, the change feels good. New start. New environment.

And, there's something else.

A guy. One of their friends, who owns a truck and volunteered to help on moving day.

He catches my eye, and I catch his, and the day starts to become something else.

A new opportunity. A new interest.

Within a week, we are dating.

We spend all our free time together, tied-at-the-hip connected.

. . .

I learn more about him.

He is thirty-one, but doesn't mind that I am only eighteen.

He's not like Derek at all.

He's a grown-up with a full-time grocery store job and a leased truck and a room in a house he rents from a friend.

He thinks poetry is lame and all that existential crap is a waste of time.

He loves animals. Dogs, especially.

He wants a family. A wife who cooks, who raises respectful kind children.

His own childhood was quite messed up, something that we bond over.

But that's why he has put so much energy into perfecting his life.

And he sees potential in me.

I'm like my sister, he tells me.

I could be as attractive as Joyce someday, if I try.

75

GRADUATION

The next weekend, I drive back to Mom's.

She and Eileen have thrown me a graduation party.

I know that they put a lot of work into this.

They created poster boards with photos of me growing up.

They made food, bought decorations.

But all I think of is you.

I will see you. Now a month old.

Will you know me?

Will you flinch away from me?

What will I feel when I see you again?

When Bryan and Ang arrive, I see no one but you.

. . .

When I hold you, I feel safe.

It's an odd emotion. Not sad, not happy.

Safe.

My worry for you, my fear for you, that anxiety that all those haywire hormones drummed up into a humming low-level panic for the past four weeks, is quieted. Soothed.

I am soothed by the holding of you.

I am careful not to hold you too long, or treat you too possessively, or stray from the acceptable vocabulary.

And when I return you to your parents, I expect my arms to feel as empty as they did when I left the hospital, but it does not feel this way.

The wound and the salve, once again, the same.

I talk to everyone, thank them for coming, tell them about my college plans. But my only memory of that day is you.

76

SHOWER

The next day, a baby shower.

Angela's baby shower.

Of course, I would be invited in any circumstance. Inviting all the female cousins is tradition.

When I arrive, an aunt is holding you. She instantly offers to pass you on.

I do not turn her down, but I am conscious of being watched, my reaction to your weight in my arms scrutinized by everyone in the room.

I focus on you for a few minutes, your sharp blue eyes watching me.

Then I pass you on to the next waiting aunt.

. . .

We play shower games and celebrate Angela and the new family she is creating.

Rachel watches me closely, looking for the crack that signals my imminent shattering.

I use the restroom more times than is reasonable, each a chance to swallow my tears and breathe slowly, pull myself together. I must keep it together.

This is how adoptions are closed. I know from the forums.

Angela has given me no reason to think she would close this adoption. I don't think she is a vindictive or harsh woman, but she is a new mom and deserves to be celebrated. She has been open with me and I don't know her limits, how far she can be pushed before she closes me out.

If I make today about me, if I destabilize the event, if I take away Angela's joy...

This is a tenuous time. The stakes are high. Every action a clue to the future and can be extrapolated, in fear or in optimism.

I must keep it together.

Angela opens her gifts, practical consumables, beautiful decorations for the nursery, piles of pink dresses.

· · ·

I keep it together, Rachel on one side of me, Mom on the other.

Angela poses for photos with you. She invites me into frame for a few. Then there are photos of just me and you.

I keep it together.

When the day is over, I head to my car. I am exhausted.

I turn on the radio and as soon as I leave the city limits, I sob.

Loud, painful sobs.

This weekend, it was good for me.

But it was a lot. It was more than I was ready for.

77

FIXER

It is a hard day.

I don't have a job yet. Classes don't start for another three months.

I can't get off Joyce's couch.

My energy, gone.

My willpower, gone.

Gone. Like my baby, gone.

Desiree is three. She doesn't know what's wrong with me and the concern is writ plain across her brow.

I won't play with her.

I won't respond to tickling.

I won't get up.

She doesn't know how to fix me, so she leaves.

Desiree returns with her blankie. She covers my shoulders, then tugs the blankie down to my feet. She frowns when she sees my bare shoulders and pulls it back up, exposing my feet again.

The gesture is unbelievably kind and triggers a fresh wave of tears. The well should be dry by now, but still, there are more tears.

She returns with a wet rag for my forehead. She has not wrung it out, and water streams down my face, into my ears and onto my neck. It makes me laugh, but I don't get up.

She leaves, more upset than before.

She comes back with a bottle of Pepto Bismol.

This is still not enough to get me moving.

Tears well in her big brown eyes.

And this moves me.

This kid, showing me love and compassion in every way her little heart knows how.

I cannot let her fail.

I sit up.

She smiles and hugs me.

I shove fake enthusiasm into my voice. "What do you want to play?"

Her smile clears the last shimmer from her eyes and once again, she becomes three and carefree.

78

GOOD DAY

My first good day happens a few weeks after leaving you.

I think of you first thing in the morning, like I do every day.

But I don't have time to lie there and cradle the ache inside me. I have a date with Jake.

We spend the day flirting and playing.

And when I crawl into bed at night, I think of you again, like I do every night. But then, I am too exhilarated to be sad.

I think of something I read about grief.

That it's okay to have good days.

That the length of time I feel awful is not directly proportional to the amount of love I hold for the person.

That I shouldn't punish myself by clutching to lousy feelings as a way to justify the depth of my love for you or the depth of my grief for your loss.

That I shouldn't feel guilty for having good days.

I fall asleep grinning.

79

BAPTISM

You are two months old.

I am invited to your baptism.

According to the official adoption plan, I am to receive updates every three months, and I get four visits the first year, three the following, then two, and then one visit every year after that, or maybe more if your parents allow. This was the compromise I made with the adoption lady. My hope is that your parents will allow more.

There are family weddings every year, and Christmases and graduation parties and baby showers. I could, maybe, see you a few times a year your whole life. Maybe.

Bryan and Angela invite me to spend the night before the baptism at their house.

I borrow a dress from Rachel and wear my own comfortable shoes.

I barely sleep the week prior.

When I arrive, I am on best behavior. Please and thank you and how can I help?

I need to prove to them, and to me, that this adoption can stay open.

That visits are happy events that we can have more of in the future.

Family arrives in droves for the baptism.

I like your church. Large and open, with a priest who knows your parents and seems very excited to celebrate the growth of your family. I sit between Eileen and Mom, in the middle of the pew, where I cannot escape.

And a few minutes into the service, I need to escape.

I can't not cry. I can't keep it in.

The tears, at first, are quiet, but they grow. I am loudly crying in the middle of this service.

Mom hands me a wrinkled purse tissue.

A few minutes later, Eileen hands me another one and pats my knee.

. . .

Bryan and Ang are in the row ahead of us. They must be able to hear me.

This is what birthmothers do wrong! This is how they ruin things! This is why no one thinks open adoptions are a good idea. I pile on to myself, chastising and berating, but not calming.

Why was I dumb enough to sit in the middle of the pew?

I pull myself out of my internal barrage in time for the baptism ceremony. I keep the tears off my face for a round of photos.

And then I escape to the bathroom, try to clean myself up, cool my blotchy face.

After church, we return to Bryan and Angela's for cake and coffee.

They open presents. Glass white crosses and religious plaques. Baby's First Bible.

You are passed from aunt to cousin to uncle to grandpa.

As the party wraps up and guests start leaving, it is my turn to hold you.

We sit in the rocking chair in the living room, and finally, finally, I feel calm.

Comfortable and whole.

At peace.

. . .

You fall asleep in my arms.

I watch your eyes flutter, your chest rise and fall, hypnotic.

I fall asleep.

I wake to your Grandpa Eugene's laugh. He and your Grandpa Jerry are in the living room, talking crops and weather.

Nearly everyone is gone.

I don't know how long I slept.

A sudden shot of fear zips through me. This is not an appropriate thing to do, fall asleep holding you at your baptism party.

Eugene smiles at me. "No one wanted to wake you," he says. "You both looked too peaceful."

Later, your dad gives me a copy of a photo he took while we slept.

It summons the moment and instantly I can feel it again, the weight of you, the lightness it creates in me. And your parents' acceptance of me in your world.

80

SOCIAL SECURITY

Three months after you are born, I receive your social security card in the mail.

Your name plus my last name.

Your number.

Your identity.

I hold it close to me and wonder what to do with it. Give it to your parents?

No need. When the adoption goes through, you will have a new last name and a new social security card.

I keep it.

81

PACIFIER

I am cleaning someone else's bathroom. My least favorite of all my jobs, the un-merriest of Merry Maids.

Behind the toilet I find a pacifier.

And then I realize,

I did not think of you this morning.

You were not the first thing I thought of when I woke up.

There were no tears, no empty ache to hold onto in the darkness of early morning hours.

I have been awake for three hours and this is the first time I think of you.

I wonder if this means I am healing. A sign I am moving forward.

I hope so.

82

TAR

Here is the thing about grief. It cannot be waded through singularly.

All those hurts, they mix up inside, a giant pit of muck to work through.

I do not have neatly labeled buckets of grief. I cannot select a specific event to deal with today.

It's all together, a cauldron of sludge,

You and my broken heart,

Social anxiety and isolation,

And the things I know about myself that I can't tell anyone yet.

And the past, the experiences I still can't look at.

. . .

I prepared myself to get over the loss of a child, but it's not that simple. That is not the only thing I need to work through, and I can't seem to separate it out from the rest.

My grief over you is in the vat, one great tar pit capable of swallowing whole even the mightiest beasts.

This is what I have inside me, and pulling myself out of it is unlike anything I expected.

I am so tired.

I cannot see the bottom, and most days, I cannot see the top.

Some days, I wonder if there really is a surface to this muck.

I begin to suspect this is it for me.

My old friend was right. My psyche will always be piss poor. I'm never going to crawl out of this.

Other days, better days, I feel myself rising, feel the work paying off.

But I am so tired.

83

JOURNEY

I can't stop crying again.

I should have it more together by now.

You are three months old. I can't stall out at this stage of grief and never be okay.

I live with Joyce and Matt and that's good.

I play with Desiree every day and that's good.

I have a new boyfriend and that's good.

My job as a maid is shitty. But my second job at the grocery store is okay. And I think I have a lead on a third job.

Soon I will go back to college and that's good.

But this still aches.

I still wake up thinking of you every day. I see your face first thing every morning. And then I remember you are gone and the loss of you washes over me, fresh and bloody and suffocating. The first thing I do every day is cry. And I fall asleep crying every night.

I should be better by now.

I remember the papers I gathered when I was pregnant. All that planning. "Oh, I won't numb myself. I will just accept this is going to hurt and I'll work through it." I was so dumb. So optimistic.

But I dig them out, because maybe there is something useful in there.

I find a sheet of coral paper with a typed affirmation. I have no idea who wrote it or where I got it. It says this:

> I will not cheat myself of the necessary time it takes to go through my own grief. Knowing that the only way to get over my pain is to go through it, I will not become impatient. To pretend that I have never experienced real despair is to sabotage myself. I will not participate in emotional dishonesty. I am assured that the strength I need to get through my pain is already within me. I will not ignore my emotions. Today I continue my grief journey, with a sure knowledge that my healing is already taking place.

I tape this to my bedroom wall and read it every night and every morning.

84

SANCTUARY

I spend a lot of nights following Joyce around the house, talking about everything and nothing. One night, I ask her why they didn't adopt you.

"We thought about it," she says. "A lot. Talked about it a lot. And we asked Matt's parents for advice. In the end, it was because of you."

When it's clear I don't understand, she continues.

"You were giving up a healthy baby. Lots of good families would be happy to take care of her. But who was going to take care of you? After you gave her up, you wouldn't come here anymore, because it would be too hard on you. If we adopted her, our house wouldn't be that safe place for you anymore. It would change everything between us, and you were still going to need help."

85

PREGNANT

Jake and I have been dating for three months.

I think back to that forum post, that one that said don't get pregnant right away, even if you want to. But, I consider it.

Jake is ready for that life, and everything in me screams that I am, too.

Get married, sure. But mostly, have a baby.

I am a mom without a child, and here is this man offering me everything I crave. As long as I keep myself put together, dress and fix myself up the way he likes, and keep my liberal opinions and ideology to myself.

86

MAIL

In September, I go back to college, and live in the dorms.

I spend weekends at Jake's place. He doesn't like visiting me at the dorms.

During the week, I try to act like a college kid. It feels false, but also happier. The schoolwork is a welcome distraction. Classes are hard, the concepts difficult, and I love that.

I check my dorm mailbox daily, until finally, finally, a letter with your mom's handwriting. I race up to the fourth floor and run down the hallway. Slam the door to my room. I rip open the envelope and pictures fall out.

Huge blue eyes stare into the camera.

A quirky baby smile.

A joyful face, so different and somehow exactly the same as the one in my memory.

Your mom included a card:

> Birthmom (Alycea),
>
> Hi, just a quick note to let you know how Katarina is doing.
>
> On Tuesday, we went to the doctor for her four month shots and check up. She weighed 13 lb 10 oz and was 24 1/2" long.
>
> We also wanted to send you her three month pics that we had done. Everyone has loved them!
>
> See you soon!
>
> Love-
>
> Bryan, Angela, and Katarina

I show my roommate.

She doesn't know how to react but I don't care. I am happy and want to talk about you with someone. She is polite for a few minutes, then finds somewhere else to be.

I ignore my homework and instead, lie on my bed and stare into your huge blue eyes.

INSTINCTS

It is Christmas.

Mom's side of the family fills a rented hall.

Cousins, aunts, and uncles, kids running happy circles across the ballroom floor.

I look for you.

I surround myself with my siblings, protected from small talk and politeness, and look for you.

Finally, your parents walk in.

I still my legs. Stay still.

Rachel looks at me sidelong and says nothing.

· · ·

Your parents hug everyone and wish Merry Christmas a hundred times.

Everyone tells them how beautiful their daughter is.

You fuss at all the attention, all the too-near faces.

I still my arms. You are not mine to comfort. You are not mine at all.

I surround myself with brothers and sisters and try not to stare.

I use everything in me to stifle my instincts.

You are not mine.

88

RESERVOIR

My love has nowhere to go.

I cannot eliminate it, and I cannot offer it to you.

I write.

To you. To me.

Page after page.

But it is not enough.

I try exercise.

I find some solace in music.

I read poetry and comedy.

But the best relief I find is with Desiree.

Four years old and full of words, ideas, and laughter.

Desiree eats up the attention she doesn't have to share with her new baby sister.

Desiree curls into my lap and I read to her.

She brings me dolls and little plastic animals and we create imaginary worlds together.

She pulls out crayons and we color together.

Desiree's world is full of laughter, full of joy.

When she's tired, she giggles and squeals.

Early mornings, she babbles and jokes.

And she laughs.

Every hour of the day, she laughs.

Sticky hugs, sweaty snuggles, and a laugh so authentic it can pull me out of my muck and I am allowed a moment of true happiness as well.

I fill myself with love for this four-year-old niece of mine and find momentary relief.

89

STRANGER

A woman has a baby in a car seat in her shopping cart.

The baby is holding onto a small stuffed dinosaur.

The baby shakes the dinosaur happily.

As I ring up the woman's groceries, I ask, "How old is your baby?"

"Nine months," she says.

I stare at her baby and try to gauge.

You are probably a little longer, given your length at birth.

I wonder if you have a toy you carry through the grocery store, a special familiar that fits perfectly in your tiny fist and makes you laugh when you shake it.

"Mine too," I say.

. . .

It's not technically a lie, but it is a breach.

I'm not supposed to call you mine.

Not aloud and not in my head.

This woman will never know.

And the words feel amazing to say out loud.

"My daughter will be nine months old tomorrow."

This sentence that feels so warm and natural to me.

There is no one in my life I can say this sentence to,

but the stranger in the grocery check-out line.

90

BIRTHDAY

You turn one year old today.

I have classes and then a shift at Home Depot.

I go to class and think of you. Only you. I can think of only you.

This hurts.

I did not expect today to hurt.

I skip my second class and lie on my bed in my dorm room and cry and listen to my old *Love of Letting Go* CD on repeat.

I can't do this. I can't do today.

I didn't know it would be awful, but it is awful and I can't do it.

For the first time, I lie and call in sick to work.

. . .

I get in my car and drive to Joyce's, unannounced as always, right at dinnertime as usual.

Matt is outside grilling.

Desiree runs to hug me when I pull up. I wrap my arms around her and hold her tight and start to cry again.

Joyce comes outside and gives me a hug.

Next year, I will know to make a plan.

And every year after that.

I had no idea how much your birthday would hurt.

91

SPLIT

You are one.

I am in college, but on the edge of college.

I go to classes, but I don't make college friends. They feel so young. The things they care about, obsess about, seem so empty. And the kids with causes, the ones who lead the social justice movements and groups on campus, they are so earnest. So intense. I don't spend the time to get to know anyone well enough to see deeper. I don't find my place here.

I spend most of my time with Jake and his friends, all in their late twenties, early thirties.

After a year in the dorms, I move in with him. And we set up something of a life.

We go to the gym.

We cook meals.

We talk about marriage and babies and the future.

I spend a lot of my time at Joyce's.

Jake used to come with, but more and more, he's staying behind.

With time, I become three versions of myself.

The college version, who tries to fit in, play nice with others.

The girlfriend version, ready to be wife and mother, carefully tending my boyfriend and home.

The family version, quick to laugh, quick to offend, quick to forgive, quick to relax.

None of the versions are particularly happy, but they are all trying desperately hard to build something.

Identity.

Stability.

A future.

92

VISITS

Visiting you is hard.

I don't sleep the night before, or the week before.

It is a five-hour drive from my college town to you and the day starts early.

I am excited to see you, and somehow scared to see you, too.

What if you are different?

What if I feel too much?

What if I feel nothing?

My emotions are most unpredictable on these days.

The slightest thing brings a wash of joy that will cling to my memory.

. . .

On your second birthday, you have just gotten over a cold. When your mom teaches you to blow out the candles, you look at her like she must be crazy, but then do exactly as you are supposed to when she says "blow" and you blow out hard through your nose.

This image cracks me up every time I think of it.

But other moments stab unexpectedly.

You fall and sit crying until Bryan picks you up, talks to you about being a tough girl, dries your tears, then holds you. You snuggle your face into his neck, your arms tight around him, his comfort offering visible healing for you.

This is exactly what I wanted for you, but somehow, it stings. I cannot explain why.

By four o' clock, I am exhausted. I don't want to end my day with you. I never want to leave.

But I have also used up all of my reserves.

The drive home, I listen to my old playlist.

I cry. Out of relief. Out of sadness. Out of joy. It hardly matters. After the tears, I feel better. Clean. Reset.

Visiting you shakes my stability. Every time.

But the aftermath, the surety that you are well, the experience of love in your home, it is worth it. Every time.

93

MOVING ON

It takes me two years to see that perhaps my relationship with Jake has an unhealthy tinge.

Two years of Mom trying to stay out of it, afraid her disapproval would push me closer to him.

Two years of my siblings trying to tell me, bluntly, repeatedly.

But I do not understand why. I cannot see anything wrong.

Eventually, I realize I am happier when I'm not around him.

I have a new job at the college, tech support, and I am happy there. Challenged and interested and useful, surrounded by people I click with.

And I've made a couple friends. They get my jokes and share my odd passions.

And when I spend time with family, I can easily slip into a carefree mindset.

．　．　．

It's when I go home to Jake that I am unhappy.

I cannot tell you what is wrong with this relationship, but I start to see that my behavior looks a lot like Mom's old behavior. Always careful not to rock the boat. Changing my mood to match Jake's to make sure we have a pleasant evening together.

I try to fix it.

Willfully hold on to my mood, despite its being a mismatch with his, and then, I see it. This behavior is not allowed from me and we fight.

I try again, share an opinion that I know does not match his. Again, he is appalled and we fight.

I try, over and over, to keep our ties strong, but also to pull myself out of hiding and into the relationship.

It fails.

He says I've changed.

I agree.

And we break up.

94

CHILDLESS

You are two and a half.

My new boyfriend of a few months is frustrated.

"You are living like you're Joyce, but you're not her. You don't have kids. You're not tied down. But you act like a soccer mom."

He's not wrong.

I watch other college kids study abroad, take on internships, drive to Colorado for three weeks to hike Havasu falls.

I share my envy with my boyfriend, my longing to travel, to explore, to be free. He is tired of hearing it.

I blame my empty checking account, my need for a good reference from this crappy job so I can more easily land the next crappy job. Always three jobs at a time, none of them leading anywhere but a too-lean paycheck.

.   .   .

"You gave her up," he says. "And that gave you options. Why aren't you using them?"

He is right. But I don't know how to do what he suggests.

How do I change this? How do I convince myself it's okay to act my age? Spend too much money at the Renaissance Festival and drink too much at a party and stay up all night with the rest of the group? And call in sick to work the next day?

I write a list. All the freedoms I have because I am not raising a kid. All the things I can do because I'm not a single mom.

Then I create another list. All the dreams, big and small, I'd like to do someday.

Live in the rainforest.

Go paragliding.

Ride horses.

Have chickens.

Get a PhD.

Build a robot.

Learn to play guitar.

See the world.

Work only one job.

. . .

I choose one to focus on. Live in the rainforest. South America has fascinated me for years and Iguazu Falls is the image I hold close when I think of this dream.

I enroll in a Spanish class and absorb all that I can. I take a Rainforest Ecology course for a biology credit. I take the small preparatory steps that line up with the goal. I don't know where the money will come from or how it will work, but I protect this dream and accumulate stepping stones toward it. I build my path.

And every day, I remind myself that, because I don't have kids, I am free. I can do anything, go anywhere, become anyone.

Every day, I think first of you. And then I quickly remind myself of all the things I appreciate about not raising kids. I am grateful for my freedoms.

It starts forced. I hunt for gratitude in my situation.

Over time, it gets easier. I notice, randomly, throughout the days, ways in which my life is easier, freer than those parents I know.

My childlessness, through forced gratitude, becomes a lifestyle decision.

95

STRONG

I surround myself with people who resonate like me.

Quick to react to a slight offense.

Quick to be hurt by a callous remark.

Quick to defend someone weaker, yes, but also keen to see an attack where they may not be one.

I tell myself I am strong. Again and again, I repeat it.

And when life starts to get a little easier, when my strength is not as necessary, my identity falters.

If I'm not strong, what am I? A college kid who probably won't be able to afford the full four years, who will probably drop out and pick up some dead-end job along the way.

.   .   .

I find ways to restore my single identifying focus point. I am strong.

I do not have to look far. I have surrounded myself with others who are comfortable in the same environments that I am.

Chaos. Heartache. Challenge.

Environments that continue to reinforce the only positive words of identity I have developed: I am strong. I survive. I protect others.

Week after week, I carry the flag for other people's causes. I defend and nurture and struggle to care for people who manifest their own chaos in the same way that I manifest this environment.

Powerless martyr.

Victim of an unjust society.

But strong.

96

MISTAKE

I was wrong.

I never should have given you up.

I could have been your mom.

We could have been a family.

This is a mistake I cannot fix.

97

LOW

It has been three years since I left you and I am not okay.

I am certain I will never be okay.

This is just too much. It's too hard.

And some of these wounds are too old to heal correctly now.

Bones that should have been reset that weren't and now ache every time there's a chill in the air.

I try a therapist, but I dislike him immediately.

I try a psychologist, but after a few sessions with her, I stop going.

Still, I know I am not okay.

At these moments, you help.

You are far away and disconnected from me right now, but the thought of you helps.

I can't quit. I can't give in.

Someday, I tell myself, if I'm an absolute mess, an alcoholic living in a slummy apartment stringing together multiple jobs, you might think it's because of you. That getting pregnant ruined my life. That giving you up ruined my psyche.

You might think it's genetic. That failure is in your DNA. You might internalize my inability to stabilize as your fault and your future.

I know there's a word for this line of thinking, some fancy psychotherapy word.

I can't remember it, but I'm pretty sure it's not healthy.

But it works for me.

Motivates me.

I cannot quit. I must keep moving through this.

98

BEING MOM

You are three.

It is Christmas, an overwhelming gathering in a family this size, a rented event hall with concrete floors, carols playing from a boombox in the corner.

I can't stop watching you.

Your curls bounce. You are in a dress and running shoes.

Your teeth are tiny. Your legs are short.

Your personality overflows.

But there are so many people.

You are lost in a forest of legs and cannot find Mom.

You are on the verge of tears when you spot her and run to her leg.

She is mid-conversation.

She pats your curls, but she must hear your breaths, sense your distress. She breaks off conversation to give you her full attention.

I hide in the restroom a moment, try to swallow tears.

It was a stupid slip of my mind.

When you were lost, looking for Mom, my heart screamed, "I am here."

Stupid instinct and now I'm hiding in a bathroom stall forcing it to go away.

From behind my closed door, I hear your mom enter, and then you, swallowing your tears.

"Deep breath," she says. "There's a lot of people in there, huh?"

You agree, more sob than word.

"Let's just take a moment in here where it's quiet," she says. "Let's calm down a minute."

You breathe in raggedly, blow out loudly, with intention. A practiced exhale. You have done this before.

I breathe silently in my stall.

·   ·   ·

"Ready to try again?" she says. "This time, you can stay right by me, and if it's too much, what are we going to do?"

You aren't sure of your answer. "Come back here?"

The bathroom door clicks shut and your footsteps fade.

I gulp big sobs, keep them out of my eyes and bury them deep in my belly.

She is Mom. And a damn good one.

And for all the longing I have for you, I cannot do what she can do.

It's not just the money, or a partner, or a home that I cannot provide.

It's more.

It's this.

She taught you, in five minutes, more about soothing your anxiety than I have learned in twenty years.

I cannot teach you what I have yet to learn.

It is so easy to see. So obvious.

She is Mom because she knows how to be Mom.

The longing lightens, a little.

The unfairness of it all feels, suddenly, a bit fairer.

I had a baby, but wasn't ready.

She was ready, but there was no baby.

For just a moment, I can feel the universe in balance.

You have a great Mom.

99

MEMBERSHIP

You are four.

I see you more often than the plan requested.

You are happy.

I am working on being happy.

I follow advice I read on grief:

> Eventually, you will want a life to go back to. Don't let the pieces fall apart while you're in pain. Keep building a life, as much as possible, even when you hurt. And if you can't work on one part of life, then build the others.

Bit by bit, I build.

I live in a cheap apartment with a messy roommate and we are perpetually broke, but this is normal for college life.

I work too many hours, sleep too little.

I make friends. Friends my age. Friends who, on the surface, have everything easy. When I bother to learn more, I realize everyone is working through hardship. Everyone has baggage. Everyone struggles with something.

I start to loosen the hold of my victim card. Or, at least I start to see everyone else has one too, whether they choose to flash it around. I'm not ready to retire mine. Not yet. But I see my unique status as "the one who got screwed over by life" diminishing. Even the shiny, perky people could be card-carrying members of the victim club.

How do people get out of that damnable club?

It seems, once initiated, most people stay members for life.

I hope it is not a lifetime membership.

100

BECOMING

The way I view myself has to change.

I cannot sustain this.

I am poor.

I am broken.

I am heartsick with loss and damage and secrets.

I am unskilled and incapable.

I am going nowhere.

I try to change the story in my head with self-help derived affirmations.

I am powerful.

I am capable.

I can handle anything.

It doesn't work.

I don't believe a word of it.

These fake affirmations only serve to highlight how far my reality strays from my goals.

Eventually, I find words that work for me. Words I believe. Words that can bully my damaging old mantras out of place. Words that I can think immediately until they become so consistent, so common in my head, that they replace those old mantras all together.

I am poor becomes

I am working toward financial stability.

I am broken becomes

I am healing.

I am heartsick with loss and damage and secrets becomes

I have experienced a lot of hurt and I am figuring out how to resolve my past and build a future.

．　．　．

I am unskilled and incapable becomes

I am learning skills and proving to myself how capable I can be.

I am going nowhere becomes

I am moving on.

Later, years later, I will reach a point where I believe that I am powerful, I am capable, and I can handle anything.

But these words of becoming, they bridge the gap until I get there.

101

FAMILY

I turn twenty-two tomorrow.

Your parents are driving through my city on the way to Minneapolis. They offer to stop for lunch on the way.

It is unbearably cold outside.

We settle in to the restaurant. You take off your hat and release a pile of soft curls, static filled and gravity free.

I want to pull one and watch it bounce back, but I hate when people pull my curls, so I don't.

After lunch, we wander the mall.

In a gift shop, you spot a stuffed cocker spaniel.

You race to give it a bear hug.

It's bigger than you.

When you step back, you see the black Labrador next to it,

and the little lab in the middle.

"It's a family! Like Mommy, Daddy, and Katarina."

The wound and the salve, together again.

You know your place. You have a place. You fit. And it's perfect for you.

And I am not a part of it.

You play with the stuffed animals while we wander the store.

After a minute, you huddle us back to the dogs.

You have found another large cocker spaniel and added it to the others.

You pronounce "Mommy, Daddy, Katarina, and Alycea—now it's a real family."

"That looks like a perfect family to me," Ang says.

I swallow my tears.

Resist the urge to scoop you into my arms.

Thank you.

No one else could have made my heart feel this full.

My perfect birthday gift—to be a part of your family.

102

SECRETS

You are four years old.

At this moment, I know with absolute certainty that I have done the right thing by removing you from the chaos of my life. I am glad you are tucked away in your happy life with parents who are not slogging through the mess I'm working through. I am grateful you are not here, to feel this tension, to be a part of what is coming next.

Life is hard right now.

Really hard.

I dropped out of college. I am in and out of therapy. I've been reading and studying and learning, and I know the damage that keeping secrets can do.

I need to tell people about my father. I need to confront it. I need to do something about it.

. . .

But that's not my only secret.

I start with the easier one.

I tell my siblings I have a girlfriend. Not a friend, but a girlfriend.

I tell Mom.

I tell them gender doesn't matter much to me. It's not criteria I use when dating. And I am currently dating a woman.

I bring my girlfriend home for Christmas.

I introduce her to my family.

My family, uncomfortable with this, unfamiliar with any of it, steps up again. They are kind and polite and make her welcome.

A month later, I bring my girlfriend to a family wedding.

In my sprawling family of two hundred cousins, aunts, and uncles, I am the first person to come out.

I ask the bride and groom first, if they would mind.

I ask Bryan and Ang, if they would mind.

And then, at the wedding, when cousins ask me why I didn't tell them, I lie. "I wasn't trying to hide it," I say. "I just thought everyone knew."

And with that, a fear I've carried inside me for ten years,

a fear I've agonized over, cried over, stressed over,

vanishes.

I am okay. We are okay.

My family is family in word and love.

It is reassuring enough to tackle the next one, the harder one, the darker one.

103

BIRTHMOTHER

A contentious title.

But what are the options?

Mother or Mom—immediately scrapped. That role is already taken in your world.

Natural mother—demotes Ang to the "unnatural" mother. Scrapped.

Real mother is wrong in so many ways. Scrapped.

Birthmother.

Others hate this.

Does that make Ang the deathmother? Does it mean my role must end at birth?

The title is the best of the available options.

But we warm up the title.

Birthmom.

That's a little better feeling, a little kinder.

We agreed on this word during the planning stages, and now, four years later, I see the impact of our decision.

At four, you do not understand.

Everyone who shows up at your birthday has a title.

Aunt, Godmother, Birthmom, Grandma.

We are women with titles who love you and bring you gifts on your birthday, for which you must say thank you and possibly pose for a snapshot with before you can eat cake.

Your aunt is pregnant. You know there will be a baby.

So you ask her, "who will she give the baby to?"

This makes me happy.

Your world is the norm. Unshakeable. Standard. Everyone else is the deviation.

This is what I hoped for when we kept no secrets, told no lies.

You are you. Your family is complex and true and good.

I am a woman who loves you and brings you presents and loves to take pictures with you.

And I am proud of my title: Birthmom.

104

COURT

I finally tell my family about my father.

And then, I tell law enforcement. I press charges. I go to court. It is all awful.

But I can do it now.

Because I am stronger.

I know who my people are. I know who I can count on to show up for me.

I know how to work through pain.

I know that the lump in my throat will fade with time.

I know this awfulness is not a permanent state.

I know I am capable of wading through the muck and finding the light, and I know that life does not need to fall apart on me while I do so.

I learned all these things through my experiences with you.

Having you, leaving you. You were the experience that empowered me.

You made me strong.

The next day, I call Rachel. "Will you chop off my hair?"

"Are you sure?" She has learned to be skeptical of rash cutting decisions made at the height of emotion.

"You don't have to. I can do it myself and have you fix it later."

"I'll do it," she says. "My last appointment tomorrow should be done by 7:00."

Rachel cuts off nearly a foot of hair and I leave with a sleek, short bob.

This shedding, this new image in the mirror, this physical change—it's deliberate.

I am done carrying my past into my future.

Today is my new start.

105

STRUGGLE

A friend sleeps on my couch, bruised from last night's fight, afraid to go home.

Another has not left her house in months, with the exception of buying smokes at the gas station on the corner. Her daughters buy groceries and toilet paper. Take themselves to school.

Another friend is relieved that her ex will be on house arrest for the next six months. She can cancel daycare now that he is certain to be home.

Jail time, just long enough to dry out. Illness and struggle and hardship and poverty and chaos. This is the environment I live in now.

At our regular bar, I see a woman who rarely comes out with us anymore. I ask her where she's been. "Home. Saving money."

I prod a little more.

"My kid is little right now, but I don't want to raise her Section 8. I'm gonna buy a little plot of land and put a trailer on it. So I've been taking extra shifts and saving everything I can. I pay my savings first, then bills, then groceries. If there's anything left over, I'll go out, but there usually isn't."

"That's great. Good for you."

"Yeah, well, my kid's happy. Since I don't see a lot of my old friends anymore, I have more energy to play with her."

This hits on a suspicion that has been percolating in the back of my mind, one I don't want to think about. I'm pretty sure it makes me heartless.

I think the support we offer one another, is not support.

It's permission.

Permission to stay exactly as we are, forever struggling, forever failing.

We reward each other for trauma. Each new drama creates a frenzy of love and an outpouring of kindness and a circle of friends lifting you up.

There is no reward for this woman working hard, staying home, and making progress. As a group, we punish that behavior with isolation.

If she were to be evicted, we would show up in droves to help her pack, scramble to find her new housing, and swath her in compassion. But progress, real progress, is shunned.

. . .

I sit with the idea for a few weeks, look for evidence.

Evidence is everywhere.

And the next step is gut-wrenching. If I want to move forward, I need to abandon this social world I've joined. I have to cull people from my world. I have to disengage. And I can't do it in stages, because everyone is connected, and one chaos-laden friend is enough to pull me back in to the thick of it.

Maybe other, kinder people could straddle both worlds. But I can't. I'm either in it, or I'm not.

I need to ignore everyone who needs help, because they will always need help, but they will never create a path out of this.

I need to leave.

I need to start over.

106

TABOO

I talk about you too much.

I open up about you too soon, with too many people.

It's taboo.

I don't care.

I get labeled as low class, lacking social cues, low on emotional intelligence. Those may all be true and I still don't care.

I know adoption is not something people talk about.

But it should be.

And in my world, it will not be taboo.

I will always talk about it because you are not a secret. Your story is not something to hide. You are amazing and a source of my pride.

. . .

So, I talk about you too much. Perhaps I have over-corrected, sharing too soon with too many people.

People tell me I am doing it wrong. "As you get older, you will learn," they say.

And I do learn.

I learn that when I talk about you, I free others to share their taboos.

"My mom is really my grandma. My sister is my real mom."

"My boy's real father split when I was pregnant, but my husband adopted him when he was one. We haven't told him yet."

"I had an abortion at fifteen. I don't regret it."

"I had an abortion last year. I'm not sure if I should have so I'm just trying not to think about it."

"I had a miscarriage last year. I haven't told anyone, but I'm heartbroken."

. . .

"I miscarried when I was in college. I still feel guilty for feeling so relieved."

"I had an abortion. No one knows."

"I had an abortion. No one knows."

"I had an abortion. No one knows."

The weight these women carry, keeping secrets, hiding their taboos, is too heavy to bear alone.

The more I hear, the more I share about you.

It is not always about me or about you. Together, our story creates a safe space for others to reveal their taboos.

To unburden their souls.

I hope, someday, they too will learn.

107

LUXURY

I rent a room in a new city, sharing a house with a new friend. I don't know her well yet. My siblings have known her for years, and they love her. And, their judgment is proving better than my own.

My new roommate is happy and stable. She is rarely home. Her house does not smell of cigarettes. Garbage does not pile in any corners. There are no mice.

My room is furnished with the thickest, softest, nicest bed I have ever slept in. A beautiful armoire and chest of drawers. A small couch. My bedroom is about the size of my last apartment.

I find a job answering phones.

At night, I am relieved to come home to my own place. To be single. To have no one waiting for me to build them up, help them out.

I thought I would be lonelier, but mostly, I am relieved.

For the first time, I love being alone.

108

VICTIM

Card-carrying members of the victim club do not need to stay this way.

I learn this, at twenty-four, while answering phones for a self-help company.

Forty hours a week, I am surrounded by people who embody self-determination and control over one's future.

I struggle at first. My company sells peak performance, prosperity, abundance. My company sells hope.

But the buyers don't call in knowing what they need. They call in with problems. "I think my husband is cheating me. What product do you recommend?"

I am forced into a new way of thinking. "We have a few options, depending on what you are looking for. Would you like to create sparks within your marriage, or perhaps build financial independence and confidence to set out on your own?"

For every problem, I see past it, to what is missing, what is needed.

There is a pattern to the callers.

I know who will return the products before I sell them.

Buyers caught in the past, stay there.

They haven't gotten over an old divorce, a lost promotion.

Forty-year-old women who are angry because their parents weren't proud of them in high school.

People who feel the world owes them something more than what they've been given.

People who think their personal story is so unique, so traumatic, they should not be expected to move on from it and no one else could possibly understand.

These improvement-seekers buy products, return products, call and complain to me about how ineffective products are. They do not improve.

There is another type of caller. They do not tell me their problems. Not directly. They say "I think the next best thing I can do for my career is improve how people perceive me. What do you recommend for this?"

"You could work on building a million-dollar vocabulary, or we have a program targeted on presenting yourself well during a sales pitch."

These people have identified one thing, one part of life that they could take a little more control over, and have sought a way to improve it.

These people improve. They do not complain to me about products not working. They are willing to do the work.

If they return a product, it is not the product's fault. "I guess I'm looking more to improve my personal relationships, not my sales pitch. Do you have something like that?"

They own each decision, even when they are wrong.

Surrounded in this lifestyle, my mindset shifts.

It is all about control. All about power.

The victims, they have in common one thing: it is not their fault. Therefore, it is not within their control to fix.

The successful people have in common something else: it doesn't matter whose fault it is. They take control of everything within their power.

· · ·

Over the next few months, I take home the products, sample them, the better to sell them, of course. I work my way through every product the company sells.

But I learn from the buyers the mindset that makes the products work.

I take control. In baby steps, control over everything I can.

I see past the problem to what is missing, what is needed. I identify one thing that I have the power to improve and I take control of that thing.

Over two years, I create momentum. I move to a cheaper place and cut my rent. I buy five nice work outfits, then save every dollar. I get another part-time job. I dig out of debt. I convince my boss that, by paying me an extra three dollars an hour, I can afford to quit my second job. I find a college that accepts all of my previous credits and allows me to take the rest of my classes at night. I find a professor who is willing to sponsor my idea of college credit during a self-created study abroad program in the rainforest. I reignite my South America dream.

The more I fix, the more I find is within my control. Free of that victim card, I am weightless. I create a self-perpetuating upward spiral.

109

AVERY

You have a new little sister.

You parents returned from China with a little girl, not quite two years old, who I get to meet today.

I've been thinking about her a lot.

Avery will never know her birthparents.

She can't. It's far too risky for them.

Her birthmom doesn't have the luxury of being known.

Keeping a connection is not safe for her.

I learn about Chinese adoptions, focusing on the birthparents.

Based on statistics, I create a vision of Avery's birthmom. Statistically, she is most likely rural, married, and poor.

Most likely, she already has a daughter. And she needs a son. A son to help run the household. A son to go to work when he's grown and provide for the family as his parents age.

Most Chinese women who are rural, married, poor, and already have a daughter, when they get pregnant, find out the gender of the baby. If it is not a son, they terminate the pregnancy and try again. And again. Until they have a boy.

Avery's birthmother did not do this.

Which means she is also most likely very young or very poor. Or both.

Very young.

Very poor.

Already raising a child.

And now, with a second daughter, any dreams of financial security in the future are shattered.

A second daughter cannot take on the role of a son.

A second daughter cannot provide for the family.

A second daughter means the family, all living generations, will suffer.

Will face endless poverty. Endless hunger.

She cannot have a second daughter.

If statistics hold true, she had to give Avery away or risk her family's future.

. . .

Avery was found in a high-traffic area, wrapped tight, with a bag of milk and a note with her name and birthday.

Avery was loved.

Avery was given everything this birthmother had to give.

And, after two years in the Chinese orphanage, as Bryan and Angela worked the red tape, she has been brought across the ocean, across the world, to a new home in northern Minnesota.

Where we do not speak her language.

Where we do not sing her lullabies.

Where there are no birthparents.

But where there are new parents who will love her, adore her, devote themselves to raising her.

I think about Avery's birthmother a lot.

Who she is. The decisions she made.

The risk she took leaving her baby in a place where Avery was sure to be found quickly, even if it meant she was more likely to be caught leaving her. Where she left her wrapped, with milk, with a note, even though all these things make it easier to track down the birthmother, hold her accountable, punish her for the crime.

I think about what I would want, if I was this birthmother.

. . .

When I talk to Angela, I make a proposition.

"I don't want Avery to feel left out," I say. "It's not really fair that Katarina gets attention and presents from a birthmom, when Avery won't have that chance. Do you know what kind of role you want me to have in Avery's life? If you want, I'd love to play the birthmother role to her as well. It's not the same, I know. But I can be a sort of stand-in."

Over the next few years, I try.

I try to find gifts I think her birthmother might have liked.

When Avery is very small, a little doll who looks like her.

Popular Chinese fairy tales that her birthmother would have known, would have read to her if she could.

As Avery grows older, gifts that suit her personality and interests, that help her grow into her own unique self.

I try to show up for her as the generic birthmom, the extra adult that hangs around and only wants to know that you are safe and loved and happy and growing into an amazing girl.

Being Avery's "adopted birthmom" makes me consider all birthmothers. I look for trends, for patterns in behavior.

I find absolutes, things that are true for all birthmoms.

Her birthmother thinks about her on her birthday.

All birthmoms think about their children on their birthdays.

. . .

Her birthmother looks at other kids her age, and wonders.

Wonders if Avery is tall or short for her age, loud or quiet, sweet or tough.

Every birthmom, every single one, does this.

Her birthmother has not forgotten.

We never forget.

I am sad for this woman sometimes.

Avery is a cool kid.

Sweet and tough at the same time.

Helpful and independent.

I wish her birthmom had the chance to know how amazing Avery is.

And, I am also happy for this woman.

She got what she wanted.

Avery was found right away.

She was taken to a good orphanage and was cared for by compassionate women.

She found a loving, safe, happy home.

And she is growing into an amazing woman that any mother would be proud of.

110

ENOUGH

Shopping for you is hard.

Not because you are spoiled, because you are not.

Not because you are ungrateful. You've appreciated every gift I've seen you open.

It is hard because I don't know you.

I don't know you like I want to.

I know you read, but I cannot choose a book.

What books have you read? Do you like tough characters or gentle hearts? Humor or grit?

I do not know enough.

Do you still draw?

The last time I saw you, art was your thing. But you change so much in six months. Have you tried oil pastels? Do you have colored pencils?

I cannot choose for you. I do not know enough.

Days, weeks, months prior, I wander aisle after aisle.

I know whatever I choose reflects the past you and you will likely have outgrown it by the time we meet again.

Sometimes I take a guess, cross my fingers, and hope I found something good enough.

Sometimes I go home empty-handed, pour myself wine and try to swallow the distance between us.

Always, you open my gifts and smile.

You love what I bring you.

And every time, I am reminded that it was never about the gift, never about the stuff.

I don't know you when I'm shopping, but every six months we meet again and I learn more. Season after season, year after year, I get to know you a little more.

I wonder if it will ever feel like enough.

111

SPACE

I hold open a space for you.

I choose to do this.

I choose never to lie about you, never to hide you.

You are not a shameful secret. You are glorious.

And if I want you in my future, I must hold a space for you in my present.

I ignore all the taboos.

When women swap pregnancy memories, when they share birth stories, and it seems women are always swapping pregnancy and birth stories, I add mine to the conversation.

I receive side looks, judgment, surprise, scorn, admiration.

I read it all on the faces of the women in the circle.

But I share anyway.

I hold that space open.

When people ask if I have kids, I answer plainly. "I have a daughter I gave up for adoption."

Some balk, some prod, most people hastily change the subject to more socially-sanctioned territory.

But in this way, I hold your space.

I share my story, small fragments of it, depending on the environment.

None of it is socially appropriate but I refuse to pretend you don't exist, so I design my own guidelines.

Through trial and error, I find the phrases that ring true without causing too much ruckus, the shortened stories that allow more questions or a quick skim past.

I receive lots of questions and have developed clear answers.

"My cousin and his wife adopted her. They are kind enough to let me visit a few times a year."

I gently correct the language as I go.

"Does she know you're her real mom?"

"She knows I'm her birthmom."

· · ·

"Isn't it confusing for her to have two moms?"

"Ang is her mom. I'm just birthmom, a woman with a title who shows up with gifts on her birthday."

I over-simplify when people over-complicate.

"Why did you do it?"

The more complicated the answer, the less I say.

"I wasn't in a good position to raise a child" or

"I was in high school" or

"A lot of reasons, but it has turned out really well and her parents are amazing."

Everyone who matters to me knows about you.

In this way, I hold your space. You will never be a disruption to my world.

If you ever show up on my doorstep, I will not have to wade through twenty years of white lies and omissions to bring you into my present. You never left it.

You are welcome in my life for as much or as little as you need or want from me.

You are welcome here.

There is a space for you.

112

HAPPY

I am twenty-four.

And I am happy.

It strikes me as a very peculiar feeling, and I realize that other people spend their whole lives like this.

Full inside.

A smile in the belly.

Shoulders relaxed, head held high.

No tears clinging to the back of the throat. No lump in the chest.

I do not take this feeling for granted.

Rare.

Elusive.

. . .

I worked for this feeling.

I shared my secrets with the family I knew I could trust and lean on, even through the hardest moments.

I sought therapy and exercise and anti-depressants. I came out to my family and learned, once again, that I can trust them to love and support me.

I pressed charges, finished court, and shifted that part of my story from lingering in the present to shelving it in the past.

I added self-help and self-confidence and my first taste of financial stability.

And now, I have big goals I am about to fulfill.

Travel to South America.

Live in the Rainforest.

Finish my biology degree.

It may have taken me longer to get here, to get to happy, than it takes other people.

But we do not have the same timeline.

We do not walk one path.

And there were many moments I thought it would never be possible for me.

I was certain, certain, I could never reach happy.

Never sustain stability.

I was wrong.

Thank God I was wrong.

Because this is amazing.

Blue is blue and music is rich and exhilarating.

Sparks fly when my crush smiles at me, and a piece of me I thought was dead comes back to life.

The sound of kids laughing makes me laugh every time.

Family is family in word and love.

And I, me,

me!

I am happy.

113

MOTHER'S DAY

I shop early for Mother's Day cards.

As soon as they appear on the rack, I search for something appropriate. What card says "Thanks for being the mom I wish I could be?"

And then, I consider even more honest cards that don't—and probably shouldn't—exist.

"To the woman who adopted my daughter, you are amazing and I am jealous and full of longing, but I am also overwhelmingly grateful and relieved you are her mom."

"Today is about you, and I am thrilled to celebrate you (although a part of me wishes it was also about me)."

· · ·

These are the sentiments I keep to myself as I search for a card that works.

Without fail, I receive a note on birthmother's day and a beautiful card. I am also presented with the exact kind of gift I crave. A handprint pressed into clay. A framed drawing with a yellow sun and perky red houses. A flower pot decorated in Sharpie designs. These gifts adorn my walls and shelves throughout my house and I am warmed by their presence.

Over the years, finding the right card gets easier. I respect Angela. And she respects me. And this is possible because we both agree wholeheartedly that none of this is really about her or me.

It is all about you.

114

SOUTH AMERICA

In South America, I become someone else.

I abandon my story, the one that follows me everywhere, the one I carry with me always.

In Brazil, I don't have enough words to share it with anyone.

I am quiet. I listen and try to hear the meaning through the rhythm of the new language.

When I move to Argentina a month later, some of the Portuguese I picked up in Brazil translates, but most does not, and again I am quiet. I again abandon my story.

Here in the rainforest, I am someone else.

I am a college-educated woman, something rare in this part of the world at this time.

They introduce me as a scientist. And I travel alone, a woman without a man to keep her safe, without a man to shelter her.

In the eyes of the girls around me, I am powerful and brave and smart and wealthy and a little reckless.

In the eyes of those around me, I have everything.

I start to see myself as they see me.

And I see they are right.

I spend five months in South America. A couple months working with conservation projects, a couple months exploring by bus and backpack on my own.

When I have settled in to this new identity, when I get home-sick, I book a flight home.

I take my new identity with me.

115

DOUBT

You are nine.

At this moment, I know with absolute certainty that I have done the wrong thing by giving you up for adoption.

I could have raised you.

I could have been a good mom.

Now that life is stable, life is good, I can see how things could have gone with us. I was stronger than I knew, and I think that I would have discovered it when I needed that strength to care for you.

You are nine and a half.

At this moment, I'm not sure. It's possible I could have been a good mom, but also possible I would never have found my strength if not for giving you up. You were the catalyst to my healing, the trigger to my growth. Without that experience, I may have not ever been okay.

You are ten.

At this moment, I have an excellent psychiatrist, who helps me see this another way.

"There was no right or wrong choice," she says. "There was no pre-determined path where you were somehow supposed to divine the one 'right' decision. You could have kept her and lived with your mom. You could have kept her and moved to California. You could have had an abortion. You could have married Derek. You could have given her to a different family. There are so many possibilities. What matters is not whether you somehow discovered the one 'correct' decision among the possibilities. You made a careful, thoughtful decision, the best one you knew to make with all the information you had at the time. And it has turned out well. That's it. That's all there is."

The best decision I knew to make with all the information I had at the time.

This phrase, I write it down. I chew on it.

If I applied this to other choices in my life, it is true there as well.

I find solace in this.

There is peace in the lack of one right decision, in the presence of infinite possibilities with infinite outcomes.

Peace in making decisions with all the information I have at hand, and calling that good enough.

No more simmering on the past, trying to figure out where I went wrong and why.

No more beating myself up for every decision, right or wrong, good or bad.

Her words, considered over weeks and months and years, lead to a new kindness to myself.

A forgiveness of myself.

Better than stifling my self-destructive internal commentary.

Better than my mantras of becoming.

Her words lead me to a new place of acceptance

of who I was then,

who I am now,

and who I will become.

116

NOT MINE

I am at a baptism when I first hear this poem from Khalil Gibran:

> Your children are not your children.
>
> They are the sons and daughters of Life's longing for itself.
>
> They come through you but not from you.
>
> And though they are with you, they belong not to you.
>
> You may give them your love but not your thoughts.
>
> For they have their own thoughts.
>
> You may house their bodies but not their souls,
>
> For their souls dwell in the house of tomorrow,
>
> Which you cannot visit, not even in your dreams.
>
> You may strive to be like them, but seek not to make them like you.

For life goes not backward nor tarries with yesterday.

You are the bows from which your children as living arrows are sent forth.

The archer sees the mark upon the path of the infinite.

And He bends you with His might that His arrows may go swift and far.

Let your bending in the archer's hands be for happiness;

For even as He loves the arrow that flies,

So He loves the bow that is stable.

The words haunt me.

I find the poem online and read it again.

I copy it into a notebook and read it again.

For years, I have nurtured this feeling of loss, because you were mine and you became theirs and this giving away of ownership was horrible and unfair and devastating.

But there is freedom in this poem.

Freedom in the idea that you were never mine.

You were never mine to give.

You have always belonged to you.

It's getting easier to see this, now that you are ten and funny and stubborn and have ideas and opinions that line up with no one but yourself.

The more personality you show, the more you that you become, the more real the poetry becomes.

You are not mine.

You never were mine.

I never owned you.

I housed you for a while. I made a home for you inside of me. And I found a home for you outside of me.

I had the privilege of caring for you for a short while.

But you, darling girl, have never belonged to anyone but yourself.

Our children are not our children.

117

FOURTH OF JULY

Now that my older brother lives in Florida, getting everyone together for Christmas is hard. Christmas requires too many events shoved into too short of a time frame. The Fourth of July, though, offers endless hours stretched across long summer days.

We gather at Joyce and Matt's, a collection of tents and campers in the yard, and sleeping bags in the living room. We build new traditions for a new major holiday: all ages softball game, bags tournaments, lake days, the annual Beer Can Opener at the local golf course where we wear our gaudiest red, white, and blue outfits.

Your family is nearby this year, at Eileen and Eugene's. You have been spending a lot of time there recently. Eugene's health is failing and time spent with Grandpa is prioritized above other events.

· · ·

Joyce invites you all to swing by anytime. Add a tent and join us. Or come for a few hours while we set off fireworks in the driveway.

Your parents stop over for a few hours.

My boyfriend, Jer, catches me standing awkwardly in the dining room. I am usually awkward around you, wanting to be near you, but uncertain of my role.

Jer pulls out Settlers of Catan. "Who wants to play a game? Do you guys know this one?"

You and Avery join him at the table.

When I don't sit immediately, Jer prompts further. "You in, Alycea?" I am grateful for him and his habit of intuiting what I need, figuring out how to make it happen for me.

I take a seat and relax with the comfort of a board game distraction. Other kids join in and we add more chairs to the table.

Next year, you receive the official invite. Come the whole time. Spend multiple days.

And you do.

My family is happy to add you and Avery and Bryan and Angela to the mix. I am thrilled.

Our families, uniquely tied, blend together.

You become part of the event.

We take a photo in the front yard, everyone wearing our gaudiest red, white, and blue gear. It is the first photo I have, the first one ever, that includes my whole family. My siblings and their spouses and kids, and you and Avery and Bryan and Angela.

One family photo.

And the tradition continues. Sharing the meals, the jokes, the well-worn stories with familiar punchlines that still make us laugh.

For a few days every year, I have it all.

All of my people in one place.

PART III

NOW

118

EIGHTEEN

Eighteen.

The magic age for closed adoptions, where files can be dusted off and unsealed and birthparent and child can be reunited.

If they want to.

Our adoption is different. In an open adoption, there is no profound change tied to you turning eighteen in a few months.

Except, there is.

At eighteen, this adoption can only be closed if you choose to close it.

At eighteen, you are redesigning your relationship with your parents.

At eighteen, you are free to decide how, or if, you want me in your life.

It all shifts, from your parents holding the power, to you.

The family we designed, the ties that cross and interweave and bind us together into a community with you and your sister at the center, it works.

Over the years, your parents have been open and gracious. They allowed me more access to you than I dreamed possible. I opened myself up to you and them and we have a good relationship. Your artwork hangs on my walls, your handmade gifts accumulated over the years live in every room of my house. Twice a year visits are happy and easy and wonderful. Angela and I exchange cards every Mother's Day, gifts every Christmas.

This is not the adoption they make Lifetime movies about.

This is good.

This works.

But eighteen, the number still holds magic.

Transitional magic, waning crescent moon. The ending of one cycle, the start of the next.

You decide what happens now.

119

STABLE

I am thirty-six.

Life is good for me now. And has been for many years.

Long ago, I reached a place of stability inside myself.

I silenced that voice inside me that cut me down all the time. I ditched my victim card, ages ago, and good riddance.

Those two changes, more than any other, made everything else possible.

Easy laughter. Easy forgiveness, for myself and others.

Good moments and rough ones, belly laughter and loss, friendship and loneliness.

They exist, but I am not their hostage.

They flow through me, around me, part of this experience that is ever-changing. Part of life.

. . .

I could never force the muck away, the old grief, the old broken bones that never reset quite right.

But I added so many good things to my life that the muck was displaced.

I added beautiful music and stories to escape into.

New faces, new friends, new people with alternate perspectives.

Travel, which gave me a new identity and made me see my story, and everyone else's, in a different light.

A hundred different lights.

I devoted all my energy to adding more good, adding more adventure and warmth and love and joy, and I filled myself with these things.

There are a few splatters of muck left. I am careful not to step into the slick or let myself sink into it.

Everywhere I look, I see all the wonderful things that I have added and life is good now.

I am married to a man I adore, who knows and loves you, who knows and loves me.

I have a few friends in my new city. Young friendships I am still building.

I have a job that has bought me financial stability.

I live near my older brother, and far from everyone else, but we all stay close.

We are family and we do not waver in our support of one another. Not ever.

It is a good life.

120

PLAN

When you turn eighteen in a few months, I will be far away. I live on the other side of the country now.

When you graduate, play your last band concert, compete in your last soccer game, I will be in Florida, just me and the dog.

Jer, now my husband of three years, will be on the road for work. Just me and Red at home.

Jer suggests I relocate. "You work from home. Go to Minnesota. Stay with your sister for a few weeks."

"What about Red?" I ask.

"Take him with you."

It didn't occur to me this was an option, but now that he's said it, I can't fathom not going. I cannot explain why I need to go, but I don't have to explain. Jer once again saw what I needed before I did, and I needed his push to see for myself.

121

DRIVE I

Mile after mile, plus a thousand more.

Red in the backseat, my charge, my companion for this journey.

I unwind the road, unspool the tar I gathered in my tires five years ago.

Sticky Tampa air thins to Georgia Mountain breezes.

Wildflower ditches fade, replaced with thick banks of moss-dripped trees.

Signs for ORANGES give way to PECANS give way to STABLES. Tennessee barns pop red and sturdy.

The gears grind.

Red sits up. He dislikes the twists and turns and angles of Tennessee.

122

YOUR STORY

I have two days to think as I drive.

You. My thoughts circle on you.

Your story is not my story.

You have a best friend of many years. I do not know her name.

When you were ten, you wanted to be a journalist. Has this changed?

In my twice a year visits, I hear your laugh. I learn your dark, smart humor.

But what do you eat for breakfast?

What do you sound like overtired? I do not know your line

between tired and so tired you're crabby and so overtired you laugh. I've never seen it.

I do not know you. Not the way I want to know you.

Your story is not my story, and it aches.

More importantly, though, my story is not your story.

I moved every year for fifteen years.

Some apartments were sleazy. Some neighborhoods were rough. Once, I had five roommates. Incrementally, circumstances improved, but it took years.

You had consistency. You lived in one home, attended schools in one district, grew up in one community. You lay on the floor of your living room, the green carpet a staple throughout your ages. You had a backyard with a sandbox and trees, deer and moose and birds. You grew plants in a greenhouse on your patio. You had a stable home.

I always worked two or three jobs, and got my first health insurance at age twenty-four. Until then, sprains were wrapped with ace bandages and health care came over the counter from Walgreens.

You went in for every check-up. You received every vaccination. When you needed glasses, you got two pair.

. . .

Over the years, life got easier for me. I was so proud the first time I paid all my bills and had money left over. I was proud when I paid off all my credit cards. When I stopped struggling. Then, when I started thriving. When I had options.

In your story, the refrigerator and the gas tanks were always full. You joined sports, and your parents showed up for games, gave rides, and paid for recital costumes and uniforms.

I worked and worked and, for a few years, barely slept.

Your parents made time for you. They fetched you from school when you were sick. They played with you when you were well. You and your sister took vacations. You had holidays and camps and a summer job at your mom's company. There was always community around to help whenever extra hands were needed.

Your parents paid attention. You had a regular bedtime and were read to every day until you could read on your own. Then, you read like crazy. You read so much you broke the school record for books read in a year. Your homework was done. You were cared for.

My love life was rocky. It's now a family joke, how low I set the bar with some of the people I brought home. I learned the whole relationship thing painfully slowly. Eventually, I met someone incredible. So incredible I married him. But the path to my happy marriage was long.

Your parents are solid. You have an amazing mom. You have an amazing dad. You have role models, who demonstrate every day how to treat people with love, with respect. You have

n effort

a little sister, and a cat with big eyes. You have a home full of love.

I had to work through some things. I needed to grow up. I made some lousy decisions and, at times, became someone even I hated to be around. I had years of depression and grief. A few years of denial. A few years of playing the victim.

Since I didn't wholly create my mess, it felt out of my control to fix it. Eventually, I worked myself out of that state. I fixed what was in my control, and the more I fixed, the more control I took.

You saw none of this. You learned no terrible life lessons from me. You saw me on birthdays and holidays and family get-togethers. You saw a happy, joyful me who showed up with gifts and attention and love.

Do not misunderstand. Your life has not been flawless.

Your parents are not perfect. Your world is not made of unicorns and rainbows.

I see in you something that aches for more, something that feels wounded. There may still be that primal wound that the books claim, that sense of being abandoned, unwanted.

Growing up adopted has its own story.

I don't know that story.

I'd love to hear it from you someday.

. . .

Your story is not my story.

And for that, I will always feel I have missed out.

I will always want to know more, to understand more, to see more.

Time does not flow backwards and there will always be those moments I simply did not have with you.

And my story is not your story.

And for that, I will always be grateful.

I will always be glad you had more. You lived the dream I dreamed for you. You had the childhood I longed for you.

Your story is yours.

My story is mine.

They are not the same.

Half heartbreak, half gratitude of a magnitude that overwhelms me.

123

DRIVE II

In Illinois, I find a cheap hotel. Red sniffs every corner, tries every chair. Disapproves. He lays his old head by the door. Patiently waits for me to come to my senses.

Five o'clock the next morning, I do. Shower, caffeine, we rob the complimentary breakfast for snacks for the day.

Back on the road. Missouri is green and wide and long. The air is rust, wet clay. Pink trees come fewer. Stolid ranch homes ramble over expansive green lawns.

Red's nose twitches at the new scents. Rest stops take longer. He does not want to get back in the car. But he does it.

Brown eyes watch me in the rearview mirror, suspicious, wary.

124

EVOLUTION

Thinking of you has always triggered emotions in me, but the exact emotions evolved over the years.

The first few weeks after you were born, just the thought of you hurt.

Over the months, it softened to a sting surrounded in worry, hope, fear, and love.

When I saw a baby around your age, I felt first a spark of happiness, then a sting of loss.

In your toddler years, visiting you was a mix of longing and healing. But the memories of you, your funny faces and big eyes and quirky humor, those always brought a smile.

As you grew into your personality, as you showed me more of

your unique self, it got easier to see you not as mine, nor as theirs, but as you.

Just you.

Then, visits became fun.

I could see you without feeling the ache of loss. Just the joy of reconnection.

I shared a little of me.

You shared a little of you.

And every visit built upon the last.

The idea of you evolved. Now when I think of you, it is not pain or hurt or loss that I feel.

It is pride and love.

It has been this way for many years.

Pride and love.

Iowa air is almost home.

End of April is mud, brown.

The AC is off.

Acres of farms, pasted in place, while I race past.

The heat goes on.

The windows sing with the wind.

Finally, Minnesota.

The air, snow mold and ancient oak, leaves crumpled under gnarled branches, bark deeply riven, lined with cracks far deeper than their Florida counterparts.

Evidence, maybe, of a rougher life, harsh times more deeply felt.

. . .

Minnesota air breathes differently, cold and dry and familiar.

Thirty years of air in my lungs, Minnesota air.

The landscape becomes familiar.

I lived off that exit for a time. Turn left there to go to my old office.

A few hours later, my old college town.

Then the city where I lived when I was a pregnant, my mother's hometown, Grandma's house on the farm.

Twenty miles more, and my hometown. I keep driving.

I reach my sister's house at dusk, pink skies and purple water.

Hugs and dogs and "do you want a beer?"

I stretch. Red stretches.

And we set up in the camper in the front yard, home for the next few weeks.

MINNESOTA

I am here.

I can't explain exactly why. Maybe it's for me, a sanctuary to focus inward. But there's something more.

A pull. An intuition. A tie. I was too far away.

You do not need me. You are well supported.

And yet, that pull. That tie.

"Be near," it says. "Be available."

And so, I am here.

I'll go to your graduation and your graduation party and anything else I am invited to attend.

No real plans. No firm obligations. But a thousand miles closer, just in case.

127

REASSURANCE

Year after year, I threaten my brother-in-law, "Someday, I'll move back in."

He laughs a false drama, "Oh no!" Then a sincere, "You're always welcome."

The joke does not die, because I need this, the security, the reassurance of home. There is always a place for me wherever they are.

128

RELOCATING

I live in Joyce's front yard, in the pop-up camper, for a couple weeks.

During the days, I work. In the evenings, Red and I join Joyce's family for softball games or board games or chilly nights bundled in the living room.

Bryan texts me. "Katarina and we would like to have you here as much as possible so we are wondering if you would consider working from here?"

I am cautious in my response. "I have my dog. He's pretty easy going, except that he's a food stealer. I'd be happy to relocate, but don't want to imposition you with a whiny beagle. Your thoughts on me plus a dog?"

I want to be a part of your world. I want to know what you

sound like overtired, crabby, giggly. I want to meet your long-time best-friend and your very new boyfriend.

But you are stable. Your world is solid without me, and I do not want to disrupt it. Not at this moment, when you are processing the end of high school, the reality of moving out.

Now, when you are redesigning your relationship with your parents, pushing away and clinging in equal amounts.

Now, when you will first meet the adult you, the you who you will be on your own.

This moment in your life is already under pressure.

But, at the same time, I want to be near you.

I am pulled to you.

I dodge the commitment at first. "How about this - Mom and I will come just for the day on Mother's Day, like we planned. Then we can talk in person and make a plan for the next few weeks. Maybe Red and I can drive up next weekend to stay."

When I see you in person, the invite becomes much clearer.

You want this. "It's kind of weird you're just a couple hours away and I haven't seen you yet," you say. "You should just stay here."

I talk to your mom. "Katarina wants you here," she says, "and I'm fine with it."

. . .

A. K. SNYDER

So, next weekend, I'm packing up.

I'll load the car with all my clothes plus Red, and we will finish out this trip in your front yard.

129
DOG I

I was nervous to show up with a dog.

Animals are not allowed in your house.

And especially not nosy, food-stealing beagles who whine whenever I am out of eyesight.

Plus, I think you're afraid of dogs, a little.

You love Red.

You gravitate to him instantly. You sit on the ground, wrap your arms around him and he smiles.

He is a welcome target for both of us to focus on while we wade through the initial small talk and settle into unfamiliar words.

The perfect mild-mannered distraction.

130

LAUGH

You are on a video call with a friend.

"Wanna meet my birthmom?" you ask. Then you dissolve into laughter.

I poke my head into frame and wave.

This triggers a round of tears in you, belly laughter and giggles. Apparently, I am hilarious. I had no idea.

I settle into the TV room with Avery, out of your space but within earshot.

You are not quiet. You cannot complete a sentence without laughter interrupting halfway through.

You are happy.

You are well-up-from-the-soul, cup-is-filled, whole-inside happy.

I suspect you spend most of your days in this state.

Sitting here, in the silent TV room listening to your laughter fills my cup, wells up in my soul, and makes me whole-inside happy.

FLOOD

You come home at 3:00.

I have a break before my next meeting.

You hover a moment, not wanting to interrupt.

I lean back and invite you to sit outside with me.

You tell me about school, about movies you haven't seen and won't see because you talk through movies and dramas are boring anyway, too bad all movies can't be sitcoms.

You talk and keep talking.

Every word fills a missing link in the past, a piece of you I long to know.

One word at a time, I become a little more whole.

DOG II

It is good to have Red with me.

Being near you pulls out the mother in me.

I want to nurture, to care, to coddle.

These have never been a part of our relationship and you don't need another Mom.

These are instincts I keep in check.

But Red, I can coddle, nurture, love.

I drown him in attention and he just smiles, unsure why he's receiving this surge of affection, but not one to question such things.

It is good to have Red.

133

AUDIENCE

You are supposed to go through photos and select which ones you'd like printed for your graduation party.

I pull up a chair next to you and we click through photos together.

You narrate.

You tell me what happened on that trip to Denver.

The thing that happened immediately after a photo was taken.

You explain which friend is which, and when you met, and what each one is like.

You and Avery both talk me through the photos from China, where you visited Avery's finding place and the women who cared for her at the orphanage. Mostly, you tell me about the food you ate.

· · ·

The photo selecting process takes us the better part of three days.

I soak it up.

Every anecdote. Every detail.

In me, you have found a captive audience. I want to know it all.

134

SPACE

You have created space for me.

Until this moment, I didn't understand.

I may talk about you too much, but you talk about me, too.

You created a space for me. You held open a door for me.

My heart is filled.

My soul is happy.

This makes every heartbroken night worth it.

Every silenced thought and bottled instinct,

worth it.

You introduce me to your friends.

"This is my birthmom, Alycea."

No one is surprised. They know about me.

I wonder what they know.

"It's so weird none of my friends have met you."

You've said that a few times and I realize it's true.

In your story, you are adopted and you have a birthmom and she has a name and a story and a place in your present, not a single snapshot from your past, not a frozen image that ended at birth, but a role that slips into today.

And, more importantly, there is a future.

You have created a space for me in your present and invited me to be in your future.

This.

This.

This makes everything worth it.

I don't have words for this. Simply gratitude.

Pure gratitude.

135

DISNEY

It is Avery's birthday.

We drive an hour to find an open restaurant that serves her meal of choice today: Chinese food.

On the way to Grand Forks, we have a Disney sing-off. You connect your phone to the truck radio. Then, Avery, you and I sing every word to every song.

The Circle of Life

Let it Go

Bare Necessities

Colors of the Wind

Bryan and Ang say nothing and indulge our lack of harmony and off-pitch high notes for a solid hour.

I heal in the commonality of a Disney-based upbringing and the community of voices that inevitably feels like home.

136

LEARNING YOU

I never thought I could feel this way, to feel as though I know you.

I never dreamed it possible.

I walk through Target and see you everywhere.

Gifts I know you would love. Things I know you need.

I can hear the difference in your real laugh versus your false laugh versus your forced or scared or trying-too-hard laugh.

Your overtired eyes, your anxious eyes, your giggly happy eyes.

You talk to me, share with me.

You are learning to trust me and are slowly showing me parts of your personality I've never seen. Depths I could not reach in a three or four-hour visit on a holiday surrounded by people.

. . .

I am getting to know you.

The real you.

And my heart is full.

Overflowing.

Hope and pride and love and optimism.

I cannot wait to learn more of you.

137

WHOLE

Losing you was not one loss.

It was and is a series of losses, empty squares in a photo album, all the moments we will never have.

I will never put a band-aid on a scraped knee.

I will never teach you to ride a bike.

I will never fix your hair or help you prepare for a recital or talk you through friend drama.

It is an unending tower of "I will nevers" that appear as you age, as I watch other mothers, as I watch other daughters.

You don't need me to do any of these things.

You are fully covered. Fully parented.

But I want to do these things anyway.

. . .

And then, through the magic of complex families and the generosity of your parents, I add a few full-color images to that mostly empty album.

You have a presentation tomorrow, and I am at your kitchen table distracting you.

Once, just once, I get to say, "Finish your homework."

And once, just once, we cook together.

And once, just once, I pick your sweatshirt off the grass and hang it on the back of a chair.

And once, just once, I play with your hair and add gel and twist your sleek curls.

And once, just once, I ask you about your break up and how you're feeling about it.

And once, just once, you tell me about a crush and you can't stop grinning and I resist offering any advice at all because you got this covered on your own.

You still call your mom for the real things.

What shoes to wear for graduation.

What college to go to after graduation.

How to deal with all this change and disruption.

She has moments upon moments, pasted into volumes of the past, lined up across the shelves of your well-kept home.

I'm sure she has said "finish your homework" more times than she wants to remember.

But I gave up my claim to every moment.

I chose this empty book.

Adding color to these blank pages is a gift, an unraveling of time, a dream brought back from the dead.

I cling to these few new moments and happily add them to my slim collection.

This handful of full-color moments, they make me feel whole.

138

MORE

I am leaving today.

I have been in Minnesota six weeks. I stayed at your home two full weeks.

It has been incredible, but it is time to go back to Florida, time to let you move on, time to start the next phase.

The car is packed. Red is anxious.

When you return from a friend's graduation party, I steal a moment alone with you.

"I will follow your lead," I say. "I will be around as much or as little as you want."

You are appalled. "No! That's a terrible plan! I'm awful at communicating."

"Okay," I laugh. "Then, what do you want? Do you know

what you want? I don't mean to put you on the spot." Before I can backpedal too far, you interrupt.

"More."

More.

A beautiful word.

"More," I repeat. "I would like more. I would love to do more."

An hour later, I drive away.

When we hit the tar, I loosen the hold of my throat and chest and let the emotions bubble to the surface.

A cauldron of mixed up feelings. A melted stew of emotion.

The only way to clear it is to let it out as tears.

Heartbreak and relief.

Connection, finally.

Then separation, again.

Joy and optimism.

Longing and loss.

All of it at once.

More. You want more.

All I have ever wanted was to give you more.

139

FREE TO LOVE

I am in love. That is the feeling.

The non-stop grinning.

Your smiling face always on my mind.

Every song makes me think of you.

I hijack conversations and bring them always back to you.

Love.

I am finally free to love you.

Walls carefully erected. Instincts physically deprived.

I can let go now. A little.

You want more.

And there is so, so much more.

Oceans of more, trapped behind these walls.

Waves of more, ready to break free.

Free to love you.

Free to let myself love you.

Free to be in love with this child, now an adult, but always my child.

I am delirious with this freedom.

140

REGRET

"You'll regret it."

I heard again and again.

The question spun and I trapped it under a blanket of affirmations.

I cushioned it with well-worn mantras.

"I gave her a good life."

"I chose this path and now I choose to love it."

"There were no right or wrong decisions, but many options with infinite outcomes. I chose one good option and the outcome has been good."

I filled my head with these words. Unwilling, unable to look closely at the questions.

Today, I know the answers to these questions.

Do I regret it?

Do I regret getting pregnant at seventeen?

Do I regret carrying you through to delivery?

Do I regret giving you up for adoption?

Abortion was never a real consideration for me. You arrived inside me as a full baby spirit, full baby soul. You were determined to arrive in this world and I've never questioned that.

The other option: Keep you.

Would it have been better for you if I kept you?

Would it have been better for me?

Bryan and Angela gave you a childhood rooted in family and strength of character and love and forgiveness. They are tough. They are strict. But they are good parents. They raised you while I was falling apart, rebuilding, and growing up. There is no comparison between the life you had with them, and the sad imitation of it that I could have provided for you. Perhaps, today, I could raise a child well. But not back then. Growing up with them was better for you.

If I had kept you, maybe I would have found my strength by necessity. Maybe I would have grown up more quickly, and maybe, by the time you were three or four, I would have figured it out. Maybe I could have had all the moments without all the heartbreak, if I kept you. Maybe we could have been together.

. . .

Here is what I knew to be true at seventeen:

I was broken. I was weak. I was living on my own and failing.

I would not make it with a baby.

There was no future for us, not together.

At seventeen, I knew only to chew on grief.

Focus on past wrongs, ache over long ago injuries.

Old pain never dies, never fades.

I had never seen moving on.

I had never seen healing.

I had never seen control over one's thoughts.

I had never seen willful redirection to a healthier mindset, a healthier life.

There was a universe I knew nothing of, where people were harmed and recovered, where heartbreaks turned into sweet old fond memories, and past events lost their power over the present.

I discovered this universe because I prepared myself to lose you.

In preparing for you, I prepared for heartbreak.

I made plans for my grief. Read books. Taught myself strategies.

I discovered a world of psychology and self-help and tools and coping skills I didn't know existed.

Through losing you, I learned I could be strong.

I learned how to laugh with the lump of tears in my chest.

I learned grief jumps from the shadows, stabs unexpectedly, and then fades away again for another day.

But the day still moves on and I did, too.

I learned how to move through heartache and brokenness.

I learned that my seventeen-year-old self was wrong.

I was not broken, but wounded, and needed to heal.

I was not weak, but young, and needed time.

I was tough as hell. Resilient. Smart.

But these lessons I learned, they started with you.

Because I gave you away, I learned to heal.

You were never a regret.

You were never a mistake.

You were unplanned, yes.

And you were the start to my new life.

Holding you, growing you, and leaving you—this set me on the path forward.

You launched me into grief and beyond it.

You bore me through the pain,

and I kept pushing for love of you.

The growing of you, yes.

The holding of you, yes.

But also, the grieving of you.

Determined to—one day—be healed.

You changed my story.

And I changed yours.

This family we are part of, it's complex.

But full of love and acceptance and most of all,

the ability to grow.

Our story is still growing.

AUTHOR'S NOTE

There is more to this story.

This book is narrowly focused on Katarina—how I felt during the pregnancy and adoption planning, and what it meant to live with the grief after placement. Of course, there's more to tell. I found a loving partner and married him, then sorted out some old issues with trust and relationships. I built an amazing career following an untraditional route. I am constantly designing this life with thought and intention. And I continue to write about it. Check out my upcoming titles to learn more.

But there's more to Redefining Family as well.

Answers to Frequently Asked Questions.

A bit of information on adoption language, including info about the outdated term "gave up". (The more appropriate phrases now are "place for adoption" or "make an adoption plan.")

Resources for birthparents and adoptees.

And photos: Katarina and me, and our family over the years.

You can find it all at AKSnyderbooks.com.

ACKNOWLEDGMENTS

To Katarina, you held the door open. All the words in the world cannot express what this means to me.

To Bryan and Angela, who embraced me as part of the family. How can a thank you ever mean enough? You made this work, and I will be eternally grateful. To Avery, I am so thankful you allow me a role to play. Watching you grow up has been my pleasure and privilege.

To my family, who has, without fail, shown up for me. I am so blessed to be a part of this clan. Mom, when I needed you the most, you didn't shy away. You stepped in to prop me up and help me through. Joyce and Matt, my sanctuary, my soft landing (again and again). How do people go through life without their very own Joyce? Rachel, for your ride-or-die support, I always count on you to be by my side. Matt and Robyn, who allowed me space to grow and pushed me to keep going. Mark, for your humor and generosity, and your commitment to supporting those you love. And the whole Snyder family who accepted everything I threw at them and embraced me in love. I appreciate this more than you know.

This book would not have happened without the belief, support, and help from my writer friends: Annette, Kim, Marggie, Sarah, Anne, Tom, Mark, Kathryn, Alane, Elizabeth, and the Tampa Writers Alliance. You suffered through so many false starts and clunky drafts, and kept pushing me. Thank you for teaching me, critiquing my work, and helping me find my voice.

A special thank you to Patty Kakac for allowing me to use her music and lyrics for the song "The Love of Letting Go."

And finally, to Jer. I count on your love and support every day, and every day, you show up. Thank you.

Made in the USA
Columbia, SC
23 January 2020